Colour me Happy!

SEE YOUR EVERYDAY ORDINARY AS EXTRAORDINARY!

WRITTEN BY
ARTIST & MOTHER
BRANDI HOFER

Colour Me Happy!
See your everyday ordinary as extraordinary

Written by Artist & Mother
Brandi Hofer

Canada

www.brandihofer.ca

Cover by: Brandi Hofer Studios

Illustrations by: Leah Dunkeld

ISBN: 978-1-7781597-2-5 (eBook)
ISBN: 978-1-7781597-1-8 (audio)
ISBN: 978-1-7781597-0-1 (book)

ACKNOWLEDGMENTS

This book really is a culmination of countless life lessons and experiences that I am so grateful to have had. Although some of the experiences were life-altering, I am honoured to share with you how they have impacted my life, in the hope that you, too, will see your everyday ordinary as extraordinary.

The people in my life have shaped who I am today—with their support and belief in the unknown and their belief in me. My community is the most beautiful and magical place where anyone can be anything and they will find love and support. My family and friends are why I get out of bed in the morning, as they have given me the gift of what it is to know pure love and joy in this life.

As always, I appreciate your time, and I thank you for being here.

CONTENTS

welcome
New
friend

Get your free download!

THANK YOU SO MUCH FOR YOUR PURCHASE! WE APPRECIATE YOUR TIME AND SUPPORT. WE WOULD LIKE TO GIFT YOU A FREE AUDIOBOOK!

DOWNLOAD YOURS AT:
WWW.BRANDIHOFER.CA/AUDIOBOOK

A Love Note to My Readers

Your being here with me, right now, reading my words, finding substance between these lines, just warms my heart to the very core. We found one another in this ever-changing, busy world, and now we are connecting on a whole beautiful frequency of these words. My gratitude cannot be fully expressed right now. My only wish is that you can take my words and start to see your everyday ordinary as extraordinary. Genuinely, I want my joy and knowledge and point of view to help you seek and find the same. You deserve to find happiness in each moment of each and every day. *You are enough.*

Let me start off by stating: I am no modern-day Shakespeare, nor am I going to pretend or attempt to be. I do, however, promise that I will be honest, raw, and vulnerable with you. And I would venture to say, I may make you smile from time to time and bring you to tears at one point or another. My only hope is that the insight I am sharing with you here will move you, motivate you, and give you the strength to make positive changes in your life, no matter how big or small.

Do you feel like you are just mindlessly moving through the motions of day-to-day life? Are you looking for more fulfilment? I would like to open your eyes to allow you to find beauty in the mundane, wonder in the stars, and adventure in your own backyard. Simply put, that beauty and perspective lives within you, and it is within reach of your fingertips.

Wondering why I subtitled this See Your Everyday Ordinary as Extraordinary instead of Transform Your Life or The New You? Because it's all about the way you view your day, how you see each and every moment. You already have the tools you need to have an extraordinary day and an extraordinary life. I want to inspire you to see it all through rainbow sparkle goggles. That's all! Seems simple because it is—I've done it, and I would like to share with you how. The more you see the beauty and express the gratitude, the more great, wonderful things you will attract. I know because I was a good ol' ho-hum kind of gal, blocking opportunity and wonder at every corner. However, the more I put myself out there, the more I put the fear aside, and the more I said FUCK IT, the more these crazy amazing things came my way. I felt empowered, I found self-worth, I did the work, and I saw the ordinary as extraordinary. And the more good that happened, the more it fed my desire to keep going, and it just keeps happening again and again. I want that for you. I want that for as many people as I can reach in the world.

> *"The greatest gift you can give yourself is to find something that you are naturally adept at. And find out a way to make a living at it. Because if you do that, every day will be a play day. You're never battling upstream. You love what you do. And if you love what you do, why do you want to stop doing it?"*
>
> – Judith Susan Blum (most of you know her as Judge Judy)

Not only do I see you and support you for who you are, I also believe that at this time we are too focused on what we "think" the world wants us to be and where we feel pressured to fit. We don't fit, and we don't need to fit. You and I are as unique as a snowflake; there is not one other person in this world that will ever be like you. You need to be the best version of yourself as a GIFT to this world. Why can't you do what you love? Why can't your ordinary day be simply extraordinary?

To start a shift and to make a change, you need to view all your life's moments as building blocks adding up to the massive tower that you have built and are adding to, to see your world for what it really is: a beautiful life that is your great adventure. You need to soak in every single moment of each and every day. Be the most authentic version of you: wear-what-you-want, listen-to-what-you-want, create-what-you-want kind of person! You are in charge of your own destiny. Hang on, it's going to be a bumpy ride! How exciting!

In this book I want you to feel free and empowered to doodle all around. Draw pictures, write notes, doggy-ear the heck out of your favourite parts. Let go! Wreck this book, improve this book, alter this book, make it into your own interpretation of this book! Love the illustrations? Colour in those beautiful illustrations. Our thirteen-year-old talented, tiny artist friend Leah made those illustrations. Kids always amaze me; I am in awe of their uninhibited creativity.

There are cues for you to reflect in areas on how you feel, or what inspires you. Cut them out and make a new sketchbook, collage book, get your own Harriet the Spy notebook going on! Share them with your friends, share them with me, keep them for yourself, reach out to me in a message if you are shy—I cannot wait see what you come up with. Let's begin!

Who do you want to be?
What is the best version of you?
What does that person look like? How do they feel?
Are you living up to your fullest potential right now?

Take a minute a write right in this book!

About This Gal Right Here

Mom of three young boys six and under—to say my day is filled with energy is a massive understatement. I get a little naked butt plopped on my face, or even sometimes, to my surprise, a cold glass of water in my face at the early hours of 6 a.m. for my wake-up call. My days are unpredictable, overwhelming, and filled with fun!

Thank you and welcome to my first book! The image I see right now is me waving at you from afar, like in *Forrest Gump*, when Forrest sees Lieutenant Dan for the first time in years from his shrimp boat, waving wide-armed, stepping right off into the ocean with full vigour. Yup, that pretty much sums my personality up right there. So excited to be here, so excited to have you here. I deeply and wholeheartedly thank you for just a little bit of your time out of your glorious day.

As a stay-at-home parent I have been through some daily shit—like literal shit smears, shit floaters, shit eating (yes, I just said shit eating). Teddy found a nugget once . . . I won't get into it much more than that (insert gag noise). I am an artist, writer, mother, muralist, educator, podcaster, and a lot whole lotta other things. I am a Creative and look forward to all the adventures that the day holds for me. I enjoy everything I get to do; my days are full of surprises. It is a very exciting life, busy with a touch of exhaustion, but fulfilling in so many ways.

Like many of you, I have had the luxury in life to have had a few trials. Yes, you heard me correctly; I did say luxury. Because those trials have taught me to grasp every moment in my tightly clenched fist and squeeze as hard as I can to literally drip every miniscule bit of substance from it.

During the highest of highs in mine and my partner's lives we also experienced the lowest of lows. We lost my mother while I was six months pregnant with our first son. To say my mother was my everything would be a gross understatement to her legacy. She was my home. With losing her, I lost my safe haven. It felt like the loss of a limb.

And tragically, three months after the birth of my second son, my husband lost his father suddenly. Two parents were stripped away from us in what felt like a blink of an eye. But we had these precious new babies that were so full of life. Like I said, the highest of highs and lowest of lows.

Those moments are the big moments of impact. They can shift one's life perspective in massive tidal wave–like ways. You can either drift down into the depths of the sorrow in the darkest part of the ocean and drown or you can swim toward the light and gasp for breath. The breath that makes you hyperaware of the fact that you need to keep on breathing in and out in order to keep on going. It strips life down to one of its most naked truths: that time is our most precious commodity. At the time, it felt like all was lost; how would we ever get through this pain? It was our children who were the beacon of hope. Their ability to live in every moment with all that they have brought us back to the present of everyday and helped us see past our grief. They were the proof and guiding light that our lives had purpose and our future was moving forward together with each and every passing moment.

Those tough moments amidst the joy will forever stay with our family. They have directly affected how we carry on and how we choose to live our lives. However hard, however painful these losses have been, I am grateful for their lessons. I am a better mother, partner, friend, and person because of them. I would never have loved so hard, I would never have savoured every soft touch of my baby's chubby hand along my face that much more, I would never have worked so hard to make others understand the relevance of our time on this earth. I want to share this knowledge with you. I would like you to know that life is simply too short. I want to help you discover, as I have, to see your everyday ordinary as extraordinary.

Take It from the Top

I am a huge believer and advocate for self-care, but of course, realistically, I do not always practise it. I feel like you can just get caught up in the rigamarole of everything and then one day it all comes crashing down, like you are trying to exit a cave and the entrance has been blocked by a rock slide and the boulders are too great to move, to let in the sunlight, or to allow you to escape.

I found myself in this situation far too many times than I care to say. But as I sit here—able to share my story with you—I am practising self-care at this very moment, by writing down and processing all my thoughts and emotions. This book has helped me just as much as I believe it can help you.

I think it is only natural to start at the beginning of why I decided to write a book. I am a painter; I have been an artist my whole life but professionally for just over fifteen years. My plan simply was this: Wouldn't it be cool if I could just be paid to paint every day? Ya, cool, that sounds like every artist's dream. Fast-forward to December 2020. I was in the throes of my 130th original painting of the year—yes, original, painted-by-my-physical-hand artwork, and I was unable to say no. I had taken on so many jobs that I was swimming in the depths of creative, physical, and mental burnout. Keep in mind I was also full-time parenting at home with three children, one of which was a newborn, so, you can picture me at 11 p.m. painting and getting up two to three times a night to nurse my little baby, Teddy. This was not fair to myself or my loved ones. They deserved more, and so did I.

This massive demand for my custom artwork had suffocated any morsel of joy that I had for my art practice and painting in general. I had earned the most I ever had financially with my art business, but for the work I was putting out and for what I was sacrificing, it wasn't enough in return—in truth, not even close. I knew something needed to change. So I decided to rethink what it means to be a Creative and how it could be more sustainable rather than draining. I dove into planning, learning, podcasts, course taking, everything I could get my hands on to expand my brand because I could not do this anymore.

Creativity lives in a whole lotta places. Creativity is all around you. People always say to me that they aren't creative: "I can barely draw a stickman." If I had a dime for every time someone said that to me, I would not be rich, but it happens so often I find it quite comical and endearing. There is always an aspect of life where people are creative: cooking, singing, scrapbooking, knitting, decorating, the way you line up your socks. Creativity is woven into the world's very being, nature, and we all are, as a part of nature itself, created.

During the 2020 burnout I think I was so far gone that I needed a full-on break from painting for a while, and this is where this book came into play. I realized writing was a creative practice and outlet I had been using and wanted to use more. I had, for the past few years, been writing poetry to accompany art and had fallen deeply in love with the written word. I also realized I had been creating a narrative for years through storytelling on social media and in sharing my journey through motivational speaking. This book has been inside me all along; I had been putting it together for years. My heart was pulling me in this direction, and it was a refreshing reprieve from painting and drawing day in and day out.

My new adventure and plan consisted of: creating online classes (which are going very well now), creating a podcast (which I am loving and is a platform where I can support other women), painting more large-scale murals (which are crazy hard but make such a difference for communities), writing this book (which you are reading right now), starting an Art Academy at our local public school district, and making artwork that makes my heart sing (and has been doing well, our new online gallery, the BHA Gallery)! Did I have a clue how I was going to do any of this? Absolutely not. But I did it even though it scared the crap out of me, and I learned everything I needed to know day in and day out, and am still learning.

As a result of writing, podcasting, doing large-scale murals, offering online art classes, educating and creating artwork purely for me, I have proudly found a little more balance in my art practice and business. I have also hired a few people, which has really helped. My business has grown exponentially and it doesn't require so much of my churning out physical paintings on demand. I am not sure where it will all lead, but I can tell you I am thoroughly enjoying my newest ventures more than I ever thought possible.

Is there anything in your life that throws you off balance or takes too much of you?

Would you like to change it?

List three ways you can start:

1.
2.
3.

You Are Enough

Be more, make more, do more, have more, more, more, more—the basic instinct of our human nature, to acquire more. This is deeply ingrained in our biology. These are basic human skills to survive things like starvation, freezing to death, etc. Gather more food to store for the winter, find the cave, build the hutch, collect more wood to build fires.

At this point, most of us have far surpassed acquiring and fulfilling our basic needs. And yet, the pressure to be more cripples our souls, little by little devouring tiny bits of our self-esteem, fuelling our anxieties like high-pressure steam until we feel like the only thing left to do is implode from the inside out. It's all we hear and ALL we consume of every minute of every day: be perfect, be smarter, be more successful, be the perfect partner, practice makes perfect, be the perfect parent, have the perfect home, live the perfect life, have perfect skin, be the perfect size. A society fuelled by putting out unattainable standards to keep selling you THINGS!

We all know that everyone shits in some kind of toilet or shit pile in the morning, at some point or another, but all we see is someone's perfectly clean home, their fancy pasta dish on their designer countertop, posing with their cool couch in their trendy outfit with their new lips, and we think *Why isn't my life THAT perfect? Why do I have pores and pimples, unmade beds, and non-matching curtains? What is wrong with me?*

Let me tell you, everyone has a boatload of issues: their dad sucked, they were bankrupt last year, they haven't spoken to their brother in years, they haven't made love to their partner in months, they have low self-esteem, they work so much they never get to see their kids, and so on and so forth. Not one person is not drowning in the depths of their being. Let's cut the bullshit and stop pursuing and browsing the highlight reels of other people's lives, stop putting them on this unattainable pedestal, and live our own lives.

I wanna be a rock star and wear the coolest clothes and la la la. REEEEALLY? Do you? Some of the most unhappy individuals I've ever met are the ones that were "living" the so-called dream. I used to work at a performance venue and I got to meet all sorts of people, some of them rolling in dough and big on television, social media, and the music industry. But let me tell you, after meeting them, this is a life I would never choose personally. All the power to the people who do, but it's just not on my bucket list. There is a big difference between fame and personal success, and of course your well-being and happiness is the top priority.

Then there is good old jealousy that creeps in while we tap away on our devices. I get it! But think about it this way: if someone has something you admire and you feel jealous, use it. Jealousy can be good. It means that where they are is somewhere where you desire to see yourself, and that word jealousy—doesn't have to be so ugly. It is just taking you on your way to where you were meant to be. We will talk about this more later! For now, STOP mindlessly scrolling through others' lives and DO something about your own. Hear me! Only YOU have the power to control this very moment of this very day. And it starts with a little of this!

Here is what we are going to work on to shift that perspective:

- Be more present.
- Make more time for friends and loved ones.
- Do more outdoor activities.
- Do more activities that feed your soul and bring you joy.
- Have more grace for yourself and others.
- Be a better listener.
- Be smarter by reading.
- Be more successful at following your heart.

- Practice is fun and practice makes better.
- Practice self-care.
- Practice having a home filled with beautiful memories and things that make you think of those beautiful memories, the memories that bloom from the trials and tribulations of your daily life.

Make some notes about all these points. For example, to be more present I have allotted time to be on my phone and allotted time for one-on-one with my children.

When I was accepted into an art university in Halifax across the country from my family, my mom flew with me to help me get settled. I was renting a tiny basement walk-in that had six-foot ceilings (which means if I jumped just a little my head hit the panels), but it was cheap and my family did not have a lot of money. I was there in Halifax paying for school on bar tips, scholarships, and a heaping amount of ever-amassing student loans.

My mom took me to Walmart to get a few essentials for the so-called "kitchen" (the microwave and two-burner plug-in), bedroom, and space I was about to live in. We perused the aisles and I don't know why I was thinking it was my opportunity to redecorate this hole-of-a-basement suite, but I was nineteen, silly, and admittedly a bit selfish. At the checkout the clerk rang through everything we had gathered in that cart. It added up to about $500. Even sharing the sum with you now makes my gut sink at the memory; I still feel terrible. I knew that was way too much. I had tried to be a bit of a decorator and added in a throw blanket and few other things that I really didn't "need."

That was way too much money for my mother. Along with what it cost her to fly there with me and pay for our meals out. But for some reason, she had decided it was worth it to be there and do this for me. I know it was too much monetarily for her because when I applied for those student loans to attend university, I had to enter the amount of my mom's yearly income which was about $23,000. How she afforded to feed three kids and keep a home on that income blows my mind to this day. One night, about a month later, I was thinking of her in my tiny cave suite and came to the realization that it was very special she had done all that for me (on top of birthing and raising me and all that). I decided to write her a letter thanking her for everything, and to share with her how much it meant to me that she spent all that time with me helping me move to Halifax (I also included a quick p.s. stating that if she ever showed my brother or sister this letter, she would pay!).

It is painful to think that just six years after I sent that letter, my mom died at age fifty-six from lung cancer. We had a year and a half with her after she was diagnosed. In that year-and-a-half time frame, my mom compiled and left each of my siblings and myself a bin filled with old letters and special trinkets she had held on to over the years. When I went through my bin, I found that same homemade card and letter I had written to her from Halifax. She had attached a handwritten Post-it note at the bottom: “Brandi this letter meant so much to me at the time. These are the things that matter in this life: being grateful, saying thank you to people, and helping others.”

I think about that letter and that note all the time. But it’s not until years later, as I am sharing these memories with you here right now, that I realize I have been on a self-made journey to live up to her words. I have been charging up a mountain to share her beautiful messages. And that when you strip it all away, there is nothing stronger than someone’s outlook and reflection on life, when that very day may just be their last.

You don’t need to be more—you are enough. You are defined by the people you touch; you are defined by the lives you impact. Likes and follows and what other people think of you are not the definitive way to live; they do not feed your soul and reason for being. You are enough because of the way you love. You are enough because of the way you laugh and cry and live.

You are enough.

Think about:

One thing you like about yourself physically.

One thing you like about your personality.

One thing you're good at.

And what do you do that makes your heart sing?

put
a little
mustard
on
it!

NEW

Mustard

Put a Little MUSTARD ON IT!

See Your Everyday Ordinary as Extraordinary

Each day I make an effort to reflect on my day and learn from it. I aim to turn what some may view as a ho-hum, ordinary day into the best day I can create using the tools at hand. Realistically, this doesn't always happen. We get tired, worn out, sick, lonely, or scared. Life happens, we embrace it, we roll with it. But what happens if you flip your outlook upside down and see that ordinary day as a day that is filled with memories you can hold on to for the rest of your life?

I was never really the "test taker" in school. I always struggled academically, which is ironic because I am currently knee-deep in course creation for a university. (To my surprise, they asked, and I said, "Sure I'll give it a shot." I'll let you know how that goes.) I would always bring my tests home to my mom with my head hanging low, filled with shame. She finally couldn't take seeing me like that much longer. "As long as you tried your best, that's all I could ask for from you," she said while staring at me from her smoking chair, from where she gave all her unapologetic advice. "Did you? Did you try your best?" There she sat next to the new black cordless phone, the kind with caller id feature, in our kitchen where she talked endlessly to her sisters every night while chewing anxiously on the skin on her bottom lip. At the time, I thought to myself, *Sweet. I no longer need to worry about tests. What just happened here . . . I will just walk away slowly?*

The power of my mother's compassion for my strengths and weaknesses really resonates with me now. No one is good at everything, and everyone is good at something. Find your thing. Find what makes you hop out of bed in the morning, and for goodness' sake, at least give it your all. YOU have the power and potential to do so; you have the power of choice.

You know the corny old saying "Dance like no one's watching, love like you'll never be hurt . . ." blah, blah! Sounds all fine and dandy, and has definitely been overworked to the point of "basic." But you can bet your ass that was my favourite quote when I was thirteen. But I honestly do want all those things in that flowery quote. Realistically, however, I have found that to live a life like that takes a few fun strategies and some powerful mindset shifts. The world is not all full of sunshine and rainbows, and the Easter bunny does not shit jelly beans on your doorstep each morning. But if we at least attempt to bask in the light and overpower our shadows, we all hold within ourselves the ability to attract more brilliance into our lives.

I honestly believe everyone has something unique to bring to the table. You have a purpose. My purpose, I have found in the throes of motherhood, is to create. In all senses of the form, from my heart to my soul to my very core, creativity has always been the gravity that held me to this earth. My perspective and purpose are unique to me, as yours is to you. I haven't always known this exactly, well consciously, anyway. Instead, I tried to fit into other moulds and I just never did fit—a square-peg-in-a-round-hole kind of situation. Or an artist-sitting-at-an-accounting-desk situation (no offence to the number crunchers out there). I have discovered this "break in the clouds" through a series of events and life lessons that all fell together, leading me to who I am today. And I am quite certain that the person I am today won't be the same person I am tomorrow. However, I vow to live, I vow to grow. I vow to accept my journey as it comes and honour the lessons to be had along the way.

All you can do is at least give it your very best to love and live every day, placing your best foot forward, being as present as you can in the small moments. I try, I honestly try, to do this. I mean, to be perfectly honest, to my ongoing dismay, shit hits the fan, or in some cases other places (as I mentioned earlier), on a good ol' regular basis round here. But heck, I am down for this crazy ride! Join me, won't you?

This BIG BOOK Adventure

Do I love writing? YES. Creatively and in the form of poetry, for the most part, because I have a passion for forms of self-expression. Unfortunately, I—and likely most of you—at a very young and impressionable age was told that I was bad at something in the arts. In this particular case, it was writing (so many times I was told I was bad). Teachers, professors, loved ones, trolls, you name it. Nevertheless, here I am, just a person, a human being, as you are, filled with fears and flaws, baring my soul to you. Because I have something beautiful to share. I guess I really thrive on proving people wrong, and thank goodness for that—for where I would be today without that drive?

I would like to throw a wrench in right here for a second and share what my cousin Kristen said about the paragraph above while she was helping edit this book:

> "Very, very few people are naturally good writers. Writing takes PRACTICE and a lot of humility and vulnerability.

> You get better by other people critiquing your work. It is HARD and people are assholes."

She is right: people can be assholes, and that shouldn't stop you from doing what you love.

I feel like this same thing has happened to many of you. Whether someone told you your drawings looked like garbage or that your voice sounded like a wounded animal and you should really stick to arithmetic because that will get you somewhere! And even though doing those things brought you joy, you stopped because someone at some point in your life made you feel like you were not good enough. Well, join me in saying a big FUCK YOU! Yes, say it with me: FUCK YOU. Now sing it with me: FUUUUUUUUCK YOU! Let's do what makes us happy, or what are we even doing here?!

Writing this book took bravery, it took time, it took love, and it took way longer than I thought it would. Will it be perfect? Absolutely not! Nevertheless, this is exactly what I will be asking of you! To take that same leap of faith, dip your toes in, open yourself to new experiences, and to do so with all the gusto you can muster!

Put a Little Mustard on It!

Muster . . . speaking of, that reminds me of the house where I grew up. A tiny little sunshine-yellow home in the corner of a crescent tucked under a forest of trees. We moved there when I was five (I'm sure because of all those trees—my dad loves trees), and it was the perfect little place to grow up. We had so many adventures in our own backyard, and I will always remember 3313 with absolute fondness.

In this childhood home we had the pleasure of sharing a connected driveway with our neighbours (not sure who came up with that great design, but great design it was not). We had no choice but to get close with these people next to us because we saw them several times a day, coming and going. Fast-forward a few years, and living next to us was a young family with three energetic little boys (ironically just like mine now) who took up camp in our driveway on a good ol' regular. They were particularly fond of ball hockey. Those boys were constantly playing, running up and down the drive, LOUDLY. They lived and breathed hockey, like the majority of young people where I am from (we have a bit of a hockey town situation where I grew up, live, and currently reside).

So, with that shared driveway all the noise could be heard inside our family room with the couch right by the dang wall! Balls hitting the wall, celebratory goal shouts, victory chants galore, and gravel crunching underfoot. Everything from what they did, hit, yelled, screamed, checked, slammed, laughed. And Sheldon, the dad, was the LOUDEST of them all! He used to joyfully growl at his boys when they took a shot, "Come on, boys, PUT A LITTLE MUSTARD ON IT!" To our pure and utter delight, Sheldon repeated this saying over the years several times. The first time we heard it, we all stopped dead in our tracks and looked at each other and laughed. Naturally, we started using it around our house too. "Come on, Mom, put a little mustard on it!" More as a joke, but it certainly stuck—after all, here I am twenty years later sharing this endearing tale with you.

And in this little reading adventure, what I will ask of you is to come along with me: we are going to "PUT A LITTLE MUSTARD ON IT!" Do what you do, be completely you, but do it with some flair.

Now let's move on to you. If you've picked this up or are listening, you obviously have enough motivation to even read a book (or at least listen to one). Great job, big pat on the back! Proud of you! Step one: check. You enjoy reading, or take initiative in your mental well-being—good job, you. Reading is one of the most explorative, meditative, wonderful things you can do for your mind. It is full of endless possibilities and adventure. Step two: you will find value in something, enough that it may even make a few positive changes in your life, yes? GOOD! This is exciting, isn't it? We get to enjoy reflecting and pondering over all life's great adventures and lessons.

But if this all moves you in some way, by all means spread your optimism around, reach out to me, share your little heart out. Because we know the more joy you spread, the more you will receive, the main message being: kindness takes less energy—you'll see.

Small Town, Big Dreams

I am from a small place in central Canada. A place where you can see your dog run away for days. As a young person I resented where I was from (as most youth often are, I was an ungrateful asshat who thought they knew everything), and my aim was to get as far away as possible and leave my hometown in the dust. I remember announcing to others, "I am an independent woman and I am leaving and I want no children," period—exclamation point (like I said, asshat). Being an "independent woman" was a great and bold statement of course, especially for a fifteen-year-old young woman in the '90s who was a bit sheltered from the world. The rest is a bit rubbish, slightly less thought out, and short-sighted, I admit. However, I was (and still am) one of those shoot-before-you-aim kind of people, which is fun and works out most of the time, well, some of the time—at least for the most part.

Back to my story. Fifteen years old, yeah . . . let me paint a picture: we just started to have MSN messenger on our big square desktop computer shared by our whole family. And about two of the kids in our whole high school friend clique had a cell phone—yes, the whole friggin' crew, can you believe it? Most of you under twenty-five will not know what I'm fucking talking about. My first email name I created was embarrassing, and it took a year before someone told me that I had misspelt it (awesome), and I am going to share it with you because it is absolutely hilarious and too good not to include in my story. Here it goes: surgarlips_4@hotmail.com. I am not sure what I was going for (attempting to be sexy at thirteen, gross), but when you misspell sugar nothing else matters in the end, really. This embarrassing bit of information brings up some very important points. It is a perfect example of how we don't know everything (and that is at every stage in our lives), and that there is so much space and grace to learn in this life. I will exaggerate continually in many ways throughout this book that we are constantly learning (even how to spell) and evolving, the world is always changing around us, we have no control over the future, and, above all else, we must take time to pause and reflect.

You're only limited by what you know now. I was only limited because that was all I knew. The more we are open to accept the fact that we don't know everything and that energy lives in every little molecule of our being and that the world is filled with endless possibilities, the more open we are to receiving all the beauty that this life will bring. And only then can we be open and ready to embrace what this extraordinary universe and this extraordinary life has to offer.

BLOCKBUSTER

In my family I am one of three siblings. I am a middle child with an older brother and younger sister; we are all fairly close in age. In my family I am known for speaking before thinking and was always the butt of every joke growing up (easy target when you act before thinking, ALL OF THE TIME). One day my brother and I were strolling over to Blockbuster. Remember BLOCKBUSTER?! Oh my gosh, do you remember?! WAIT! I cringe at the fact that I might have to explain this to some. If you are not up on Blockbuster, well, let me tell you (you bright-eyed youngster!). It is a place where us "old folk" went to rent movies or video games, like a physical place (back in the day, that is). We would drive, bike, or walk ALL the way to Blockbuster to browse the aisles to find a DVD or, for the real oldies, a VHS. THEN we proceeded to drive, bike, or walk ALL the way home carrying our treats and movie in a plastic bag. We then proceeded to watch said movie, the whole thing at once, that same evening. Let me tell you, it was a lovely place to start off a date; in fact, I wish this still existed so my husband and I could spend an hour browsing the aisles together, fight about which movie we should get, finally come to a compromise (meaning he would give up and we would go with my choice), grab some peanut M&M's, and liquorice at the till, and be on our way. We would sit and actually watch this movie together because we would have to return it in two days' time. I cannot remember the last time my partner and I even finished a whole movie together. Oh my, times have certainly changed, along with our attention spans, ugh.

Okay, back to my story about speaking without thinking. With my bro (not on a date). Picture this: my brother and I were outside of Blockbuster, strolling past all the movie posters in the windows before entering. We get into the store and I state loudly, "Who in their right mind would call a movie Monster Balls?!" Here we go again, blunder blunderson. I might have to further explain to the youngsters reading this that the movie was actually a very serious one starring Charlize Theron, and it was rightly titled *Monster's Ball.* My brother, of course, laughed loudly and proceeded to correct me. And that, my friends, is the ebb and flow of my relationship with my two siblings growing up. It never felt great at the time, and I always wanted to be taken seriously (and still do), and that rarely happened, given my bad habits of innocently speaking my mind on a regular basis.

However, I did learn a valuable life lesson: you have to laugh at yourself, you really do, or everything will be much more difficult, and not very fun, actually.

Finding the humour and joy in life is way more fun than being a dud, period. Making a few mistakes and major blunders is just part of human nature; it's an easier pill to swallow, we are all in the same boat, after all.

Life is short—we need not take it seriously, seriously!

> *"You have to laugh at yourself because you'll cry your eyes out if you didn't."*
>
> – Indigo Girls

One of my most unforgettable mix-ups would have to be the story of my first dinner with my future in-laws. This story always makes me laugh, but also cringe a little. But in the end, the overwhelming joy takes precedence and reminds me fondly of the warm-hearted, playful man who raised my husband. My then-partner and I were maybe on our third date at the time, and his parents had us over for a BBQ in their backyard.

Let me paint the full picture of this moment in my life for you. I had a black-hair-dyed faux-hawk and a lip ring at the time, and dinner with parents didn't exactly fit into my comfort zone. But I liked this guy (really liked him) and his parents were the nicest people I had ever met. I actually recall coming home that summer, in particular, declaring that I was in search of a fling, knowing I was moving across the country in two months to university. (I am also aware that my now mother-in-law will be reading this . . . cool, cool, cool.) Not exactly an "introduce the parents" kind of situation I had in mind. Back to us not knowing everything, and you never know the significance of the moment you are currently living in. Heck, this particular moment led to a lifetime partnership and a family . . . who would have guessed that at the time!? Certainly not me.

Okay, so back to the outdoor dinner. Imagine us all sitting there together at a small 4-foot round table in the backyard. It was just me and him and his parents. Being knee-deep in infatuation (you know, the time where you can't get enough of each other and make other people live through your insufferable googly eyes—ya, that was us), I was rubbing my newfound love's foot beneath the table all throughout dinner, winking at him, basking in the glory of young love. I just had to touch him every second of every day, even if we were dining with his parents. (Ironically, now if his elbow goes over the side of the bed in the middle of the night I make sure to remind him in the morning to stay to his allotted side.)

Nearing the end of finishing our meal, I looked over at him and noticed that he was 100 percent NOT wearing socks. I then thought to myself, *Hmm, that is certainly strange . . . I could have sworn I felt a sock with my toesies.* I then looked over to his dad's feet, and he definitely WAS wearing socks. Things started to unravel in my brain. I broke into a sweat and panic set in. Inner monologue: *AHHH! NOOOOOOO! What in the great fuck? Whhhhhhy do I always do shit like this!?!? I HAVE BEEN rubbing a socked foot all night . . . and it was his friggin' dad's foot, suuuuper. . . .*

Shocked and at a loss for what to say, really, I looked up at everyone and just said, "OH MY GOSH!!!"

I was completely mortified! I had been playing footsies with this old man (not that old, but old to a twenty-year-old) who I barely knew, all friggin' night! FUUUUUCK.

He smiled widely, waggled his eyebrows, and laughed loudly. Whether he enjoyed it or just wanted to save me from embarrassment or maybe just a bit of both, we still, to this day, do not know!

However embarrassing at the time, now it seems so inconsequential. And it turned out to be the best story that always gets a laugh at a family dinner. Everything in the moment really can seem dramatically different. Like our life cannot continue, and how can we ever recover from this? Just know that life is constructed of many tiny building blocks that all come together to be something so much bigger. Life is just a little more fun if we learn to laugh at ourselves now and then.

cut
out
the
Cheddah!

Cut Out the Cheddah!

Cheeselusions: Let It Go!

Are you ready for change? Are you ready to open your mind? Are you ready to join me in seeing your everyday ordinary as extraordinary? Jump in, my friend!

To begin, you must make space to let in the magic. That's right, the magic that sits in front of your very eyes every single second of every single day. To make space you must let go of all the things holding you back, such as anxieties and fears and things from the past. We are going to blow off those clouds hanging over your head, blocking the sun that is meant to shine on your beautiful face. I am not asking you to ignore these issues and emotions that demand to be felt. They need to be acknowledged and dealt with. However, if we linger too long on our traumas, they will take hold of us and pull us into their depths deeper and deeper until it is almost impossible to not drown. I know this; I have travelled down into these depths and fought hard tooth and nail with all I had to swim back to the light.

Time naturally heals, and we do need to give everything the proper time and space it needs. In some cases, these traumas can sneak back up on us at any point and time (sometimes unexpectedly). What are we going to do with these situations? Let's call them "Cheeses." (Not to be confused with the cheese you love to eat, if you're into cheese—it's a metaphor of sorts.) Let's cut out the cheddah! Yes, that seems appropriate. Cutting out the stuff that no one needs but we all tend to overindulge in every now and then. CUT OUT THE CHEESE! We all love to stuff our faces with the negative cheeses of life. And when you are so full from the cheese tray you shoved down your gob, there is no room for the beautiful dinner you've spent all day preparing!

You all know what I'm saying, right?! This is not a food-based diet; it is a diet of the toxic parts of your life. It is you enjoying dining with the finer things in life. Instead of lingering over the negative cheese tray set out before you, tempting you with all its ooey-gooey goodness, but which will ravage you with GAS! You need to leave room for what you can let in every day that will fill you with joy and sustenance—the GOOD stuff! Don't indulge the cheese monster that makes you curl over and toss and turn with stomach cramps all night (I am clearly the lactose intolerant one here).

The cheese monster is: a terrible co-worker, the person who cut you off in traffic, the job you loathe, the creepy boss, the way you criticize yourself, a shitty friend, a toxic relationship. I could very much go on here, because this cheese monster has many forms. You can't give the cheese your time and mind space. That is your energy to hone—own it! You deserve to be loved; you deserve to be happy. You need that room inside yourself open for the beautiful opportunities that are going to grace your days, even the ordinary ones. Why ordinary? Because every day is ordinary, but all those ordinary days can add up to an extraordinary lifetime of memories and joy and love.

Cutting out the cheese is no easy feat. You have to *want* to make space for change; you have to put in the effort. This is not an easy path; it takes, dare I say it, discipline. (Don't let that word scare you; it is a good word and you have the ability to create healthy habits in your life with a little bit of it.) Are you ready to quit eating cheese (i.e. stop wasting time on bad stuff to make more room for good stuff)? Oh gosh, THAT in itself is going to be damn near impossible and take great effort and control—yes, yes, it is. I am going to be completely frank and upfront with you (like I haven't been thus far): this is only a guide, a formula that I am continually working on each and every day. I only hope it will work for you too. It is a theory, a mantra, a literary inspiration of sorts. Let me tell you that thus far it's worked out pretty darn well. I am happy, I am surrounded by people I love and who love me, and the ability to create endless opportunity lives and flows within me. You, too, can have all these things, because you are worthy of love.

I also sincerely apologize to cheese . . . don't stop showing up on my pizza, please.

Just so you don't think I am a saint when it comes to dietary discipline, I have been lactose intolerant since I was a screeching infant. And it has not prevented me from consuming a pizza with cheese on it. That gooey deliciousness trumps gas pain any day of the week. One time I tried that fake cheese shit, and I would rather eat a dirty sock from my husband's hockey bag (insert green puke emoji here).

Love Yourself

You put junk in your body, you will feel like junk. Easy. Not that easy, but pretty much sums it up, period. I am not going to elaborate too much on this; if you give it just the slightest room for thought, it is a pretty simple concept to wrap your head around. We are constantly told what not to do. This one is pretty punch-you-in-the-face, soooo . . . obvious. You drink too much alcohol, you will most likely throw up; you throw up and feel terrible for twenty-four—or more—hours. You have too much coffee, your hands will start to shake and you are an anxious mess.

You eat fast food more than you'd like to admit, or crush a family-size bag of chips before bed because you're anxious and stressed. Your body is your temple and all that! End of chapter. . . .

I wish I could say it is that easy, but as we all well know, addiction is, well . . . a part of our lives. We are all addicted to something, in some form or another, or have a plethora of bad habits, but self-deprecation is definitely not the answer. It is when you actually harm yourself or others that your addiction or habit becomes an issue. It took me far too long, and with many mistakes, to realize that I cannot drink alcohol and it was self-destructive behaviour and a mask. A Band-Aid on a bullet hole. A way to numb my problems and not deal with some things I was facing in my early twenties.

At that time in my life I was sexually harassed for two years. It left me hopeless and angry. I reported it; nothing happened. No one else came forward out of eleven women. I gave names, numbers, dates, yet no one came forward. I was frustrated, powerless. But the way I was hurting and how I dealt with it through alcohol abuse had become a big problem, one that I could no longer ignore. I was at the lowest of lows. The moment when I realized why I was hurting myself, and that it was through drinking, that became the tipping point of my leaving that harmful environment. I quit the job and I quit drinking and sought help, and I took it all very seriously, because the alternative was not an option. And all that took was a decision—the decision that I no longer wanted to feel the way I felt and I loved myself. I wanted more. I no longer wanted to be in the place I was. I was worth more than that. It was not easy and it was a journey; it took many years to come to that realization.

People I was closest to did not believe me when I told them I needed help with my feelings of anger and the eventual depression as a result of what happened. I was so clever at hiding my pain and closing my drinking behind doors that when I finally hit my lowest, I had to pull myself out. No one else could do this for me. They could support me, but they could not do it for me. It took work, years of it, and it still takes work every day.

The first step is asking for help, like a doctor, a psychiatrist, then a psychologist or a naturopath, or a group, whatever path you are choosing it will be the right one for you, moving forward. If something is happening to you, if something has happened to you, reach out, reach out, reach out, ask for help. You are worthy of love and that starts with loving yourself. And it continues with you loving yourself and taking care of yourself.

The biggest thing that has helped me with depression, anxiety, stress, and addiction has been waking up and moving my body. If you feed your body and mind well, things should get a whole lot easier from there, I assure you. You've got this. Most importantly, remember: there can be no light without the dark, and by only accepting that they both live within you can you move forward. This is not about cutting anything out or self-deprecation. It is about finding balance, finding what works for you, sticking with it consistently, and developing healthy habits.

Whatever your pain, whatever your journey, there are people who will help you. Places where you can find support. There is light in your dark. Love yourself.

Balance

The Dark by Lemony Snicket is one of the books I avidly read to my children. The message of this text resonates with me deeply and reminds me that life has a way of balancing itself out, and though it is not always easy, it is necessary.

> *"You might be afraid of the dark, but the dark is not afraid of you. That's why the dark is always close by. The dark peeks*

> *around the corner and waits behind the door, and you can see the dark up in the sky almost every night, gazing down at you as you gaze up at the stars."*[1]

If I had not experienced the loss of a parent leading up to my journey through motherhood, I know I would not view my experiences of being a mother in the same way. I am a better mom because of that loss; the experience taught me the most valuable lessons about time (you know, how we don't have an endless amount of it, and that life is short and all that!). If we had not then again experienced the loss of another parent after the birth of our second child, life would be different again. I would not have my newfound relationship with my own father and he would not have the same amount of dedication to being a grandpa. We needed help—I NEED help (these boys are crazy)—and he stepped into the role with flying colours and vigour. As we all know, it takes a village to raise a family.

Life is full of balance and lessons. Those heavy losses made us more resilient and more conscious of each present passing moment of each and every day. Of course, I would have much preferred my children's grandparents in our lives; however, I don't discount the lesson and know that some things are just beyond my control. I think about them often, but not too much—to dwell on the impact of losing them both would cause me to drown in my own sorrows, and that is not fair to myself or my family.

Without loss, I wouldn't have come to know the value of love and time. Without shitty relationships, I wouldn't know what real love feels like. Without depression, I wouldn't know what it is to maintain a healthy balance for my body and my mind. Without having entry-level jobs or struggling in my career, I wouldn't know what it feels like to

---

[1] Lemony Snicket, *The Dark* (New York: Little Brown and Company, 2013).

thrive as an artist. There is a constant striking of balance surrounding us. The earth is a living being filled with energy and wonders of balance.

The perfect example of nature striking balance and birth from destruction is pine trees. You know those little cones that litter the ground below them? I am sure you've come across these cones lying on the pine needles coating the floor of a forest that smells of earth and acid and is as red and flaming as the planet Mars. My boys love to collect them when we walk through the forest in the summer months, and one always seems to find its way into my minivan. Well, fun fact: certain species of pine produce these cones that are covered in a wax-like substance, and they require the heat of a forest fire to release their seeds. These trees are literally rebirthed after the aggressive forest fire tears through their very being. The fire is a way of the forest restarting. A balance. Though aggressive, it is essential; forests can be overtaken with insect and disease outbreaks this is a form of regeneration.

How would we know joy without sorrow, and how would we know love without loss? You will be reborn from these heavy experiences, and you will come out more resilient and more alive than ever before, newly refreshed and restored. Let your light explode from the dark and relish the beauty of it all. But learn that with that beauty, you're required to accept the dark as your balance and your friend. Welcome it with open arms and an open heart.

In the movie *Shang-Chi and the Legend of the Ten Rings* the mother of the main character says to her son, "Shang-Chi look into your heart, the light and the dark. To know yourself, you must face them both."

Energize!

Charge your batteries! Now, I am not going to dive too hard into this, by all means—I am not a health professional. I am just simply speaking from my personal life experiences here.

I began running when I was fourteen. Why? Because I had some beans to burn, like major ones. I'm pretty sure these arrived about the same time my cycle did—hormones, cool. Even in my youth, I had the self-awareness to realize that my body needed to move, not just for the physical benefits but for the mental. I was angry and hormonal, and soon discovered I was a little less angry and hormonal after I went for a quick jog. I would load up my Discman with a CD and run and run and run. I always saw this lady around our town out running every day. I always thought, *She gets it . . . that is how she thrives; running is what this woman is passionate about,* and she was devoutly dedicated. Rain or shine or -47 degrees Celsius (it gets so effing cold where I live), she just had to run; running was her "thing." I get it too—I am a more pleasant individual and more fun for others to be around when I run and create.

Not only should you move, but you should preferably move outside if you can. We were not made to be trapped within four walls. We instinctively crave fresh air and light, and to feel the dirt on our hands, and sun on our faces, and taste the fresh ocean water on our tongues. (I live in the prairies but would like to visit the ocean more. I dream of it; leave a positive review so more people buy this book and I can take a holiday, deal? Thanks! Appreciate it, friend.) Now, I really don't care how you choose to charge your life through movement. I just ask that you simply do it, anytime, as many times a week as you can. Start with just ten minutes a day and keep stretching that time. You'll know when to increase your time because your ten minutes won't seem hard anymore, you move up to fifteen or twenty minutes and so on and so forth. Whether you are into gardening, yoga, swimming, weight lifting, cross training, aqua-sizes, dancing, the sky's the actual limit! As the Nike slogan goes, "just do it!" You will start, and it may seem a bit weird or challenging at first. But after a little while it will just be something you do. "Oh yeah, I'm an avid salsa dancer," or, "I joined a walking group and my friends and I head out three days a week; I wouldn't want to disappoint my group by not being there."

What activities do you love most to get your body moving?

In my experience the mornings are best, because it is done and over with for the rest of the day and I can move on. There may be a better time for you to fit in your movement—I want this to be the best time for YOU, so that you can stick to a routine. But the way I see it: You hop out of bed and put those workout clothes on— or tie up those walking shoes. You have no choice but to tackle it, because you are in a time crunch to get to the rest of your stuff for the day. Trust me, the more you put it off, the less likely it will happen. Once your movement is done, you can take comfort in the fact that for the rest of the day you get to continue to be the charming, happy, energized self that you and others deserve to be around.

What is equally as important as moving your body, maybe even more so, is rest.

Oliver Burkeman wrote his last article in the *Guardian* in 2000, and what an epic mic drop it was! Especially this particular point about time. You will never check all the tasks off your lists, because you will always generate more. We always "feel" like we will run out of time. Inevitably we all do. But what if we chose to enjoy the things that mattered the most? Here is what Oliver declares in his last hurrah:

"There will always be too much to do – and this realisation is liberating. Today more than ever, there's just no reason to assume any fit between the demands on your time – all the things you would like to do, or feel you ought to do – and the amount of time available. Thanks to capitalism, technology and human ambition, these demands keep increasing, while your capacities remain largely fixed. It follows that the attempt to 'get on top of everything' is doomed. (Indeed, it's worse than that – the more tasks you get done, the more you'll generate.)

The upside is that you needn't berate yourself for failing to do it all, since doing it all is structurally impossible. The only viable solution is to make a shift: from a life spent trying not to neglect anything, to one spent proactively and consciously choosing what to neglect, in favour of what matters most."[2]

Are we not here to delight and indulge in this wildly wicked, beautiful world and bask in all its wonders? Yes, but mindlessly taking anything to the extreme will inadvertently push one over the edge. I know I stated earlier that I love lists, and it is delightful to have the ability to cross tasks off. However, I do believe in balance and self-care; these factors trump most everything. If you are unable to take care of yourself, how will you take care of others?

We need to be conscious of where we put our energy and time, and that shall not be focused on what we *think* we should be doing while we are doing the doing. Ya know? Be here, right here, right now. Be here in this extraordinary miracle of existence.

---

[2] Oliver Burkeman, "Oliver Burkeman's last column: the eight secrets to a (fairly) fulfilled life," *Guardian*, September 4, 2020, https://www.theguardian.com/lifeandstyle/2020/sep/04/oliver-burkemans-last-column-the-eight-secrets-to-a-fairly-fulfilled-life.

Sometimes I get myself all wrapped up in what I "have" to get done for the day. And what I should really be doing is seeing my life around me: Wow, look at my beautiful home I built with my partner. It is extraordinary, and our family is growing together in this home. While I soak my hands in the bubbly, warm water at the sink and stare out the window, I think it sure is a nice day . . . wouldn't it be great to go for a walk with my youngest son, Teddy, at the park? So we did. What a lovely day that was. Teddy and I hiked through the forest and he came within 2 inches of a monarch butterfly on the tree in the woods. We discovered things together and I got to reconnect to the simplicities and meaningful moments a day can hold.

Today I want you to watch out for ways you can slow down in a day and reconnect to the moment.

FUCK it! eat ALL the cookies!

New
[Black]
BEANS

Fuck It! Eat ALL the Cookies!

Fuck It! Eat ALL the Cookies!

When it comes to eating, well, it's really you who knows your body best—you are the expert on you, after all. For example, one thing I know with great certainty about myself is that I really love me an oatmeal chocolate chip cookie once or twice a day. And that sweet morsel is something I will just never be giving up! I remember hearing an interview with Victoria Beckham in which they asked her if she ever ate cookies. (Which makes me think, has anyone asked her husband that? What an absurd question.) But they did ask, and she did answer. "Never," she replied. I was like, never? How can she continue to live this cookieless life? That is just not a life worth living, if you ask me.

It's just one of those things for me, I guess. I love eating in general and take pride in being deeply conscious about what I feed myself. Eating is one of life's greatest pleasures. I like cookies—that we know now. Do I need cookies? How can I make this work so I am not feeling like garbage because of overindulgence in the sweet suckers? I will tell you, I started making these healthier cookies every week (like a super-sized cookie-sheet full) and keep them in my freezer, and I eat about two or three a day (notice how this number keeps increasing the more I keep explaining my cookie-eating habit). I don't feel any guilt about eating them. Why? Because they are filled with a shit-ton of shit that is good for you and makes you shit! Shit, I said it again.

Once I had an appointment with a nutritionist. She told me I needed more protein in my diet all throughout the day and suggested I add a can of black beans to my poop cookie recipe. I thought, *Hmmm, yuck, but I guess they make those black bean brownies and those are amazing*, so I gave it a shot. Holy moly, I couldn't even tell the difference. Now I have a well-balanced day, eat my cookies, and get my black beans in too! Zero guilt, zero shame. I need a butt-ton of energy as a nursing mother, so this was the quick fix I needed in between meals. Also, chocolate . . . love me some chocolate. Dessert that tastes good, makes you feel good, and is good for you too—what more could you ask for!?

And drumroll please . . . here is my all-time favourite and famous recipe for endless energy and regular bowel movements! WARNING: if you feed to friends or eat yourself you will need to be near a bathroom facility. Kids will also eat these within twenty-four hours from your freezer, so parents beware!

Brandi's Cookies (otherwise known as POOP COOKIES)

If you are like me, you will flop all these things into a giant mixing bowl without measuring and hope for the best. If you aren't like me and love to measure, here are the approximate kinds of things I throw in (there is a lot of wiggle room with these). Have fun! BONUS: they are gluten-free, can be made nut-free or vegan, and are full of protein and other good things that ultimately . . . make you poop (how many times can I talk about poop in one book and still have it be okay?).

WET

1 can of black beans with juice
2 eggs (take out for vegans or substitute flax eggs)
½ tsp salt
1 cup of sugar (or any sugar substitute: coconut sugar, honey, and maple syrup are my favourite)
6 dried dates (if you have them . . . if not, fuck it, but they make them chewy and more delicious and add sweetness)
1/3 cup nut butter (any kind)
¼ cup of butter (take out for vegans, sub other oil, I do coconut oil)
¼ cup hemp hearts
¼ cup chia seeds

Blend with that blender stick-thing immersion blender (if you don't have one, you need to get one). BLEND until the cows come home!!!

DRY (stir in separate bowl)

½ cup almond flour
½ cup unsweetened coconut, shredded
¼ cup sunflower seeds
¼ cup pumpkin seeds
¼ cup cashews*
1 cup oats
1 cup dark chocolate chips
**You can take away or add any other kind of nut. My favourite thing is to add cashews because they are amazing!*
And if you are a weirdo, you can ruin this recipe with raisins.

Combine the two bowls of ingredients. Do not overmix. Scoop with a teaspoon as many as you can onto a cookie sheet (they don't melt down), and bake for 14 to18 minutes or until golden brown. Eat warm or let them cool and stash them in your freezer.

Give or take any of these ingredients—get creative, trust me you can't screw up this recipe! I make about sixty of these on a big cookie sheet, placing them very close together because they don't melt down. We keep them in the freezer. For some reason they are the BEST that way! I have four boys in the house and these are gone in forty-eight hours (to my utter dismay)! The most amazing part is that I eat these instead of reaching for junk and they keep this busy Mama's energy high because they are packed full of protein and other good stuff! Enjoy! I hope that's everything! Good luck to you.

Sleep Is Your Mission and Your One Mission Only

The list of benefits of sleep could go on forever. You are in a better mood, you are more likely to keep a healthy lifestyle, you are kinder, more fun, more focused, more energized, and you lower your risk for major health issues like heart disease. Shall I go on? That is a whole lotta of good things that fall into the get-the-fuck-to-bed category. I know, I hear you: this is my nightly me time, just one more episode (or two, or four), and before we know it, we are so overtired we cannot fall asleep. I want you to give yourself the very best chance to live your everyday ordinary life as extraordinary, and that, my friend, comes down to the good ol' ZZZ's. I now have a fancy new watch that allows me to view my sleep stats, step count, and so much more, and I do like it, because I love to win (who doesn't), and I am a killer sleeper. I always "out sleep" my husband, hands-down, and it somehow feels victorious, even though neither of us can control the whole sleep thing that much. But I have always been stronger at it than him because I have had the same routine for bedtime from childhood. But he is the reason we have these darn new fancy watches that record your daily data and sleep in the first place, and I will tell you why. . . .

My husband and partner in crime was not a big sleeper, or gave little to no shit if he got any. I was always in awe of how little sleep he required to function on a daily basis. He is a diehard hockey fan and would go out late in the evening to play recreational hockey and come home very late and watch his recorded hockey game afterward. He would then head to bed around 1 a.m., and wake up at 7:30 a.m. I know, right? WTF? Meaning he would only get about five to six hours of sleep. This whole routine may have made sense to a singleton, but it most definitely was not sustainable for a parent of multiple children. Children who are known to, you know . . . not sleep and wake you up several times a night. Here was my husband, stuck in the routine of a young and energetic twenty-something, thinking he could live through the sleepless nights of parenthood unscathed. Boy, was he ever wrong.

Our third little baby boy Teddy was born early September 2019, and though we were, as a family, over-the-moon in love with Baby Teddy, we were pushed past all and every mental limit we had. We had, after all, already been through and are currently going through five years of not-great sleep up until the birth of our Teddy Bear. No matter what sleep training we did. Kids wake you up, they get sick, they have to go to the bathroom, they are scared, and so on and so forth. We don't sleep perfectly through the night as adults. Why should we expect our children to? We are their comfort and safe space, and they come to us for their needs—how can we be mad at that?

We knew that at least one of those other effers was going to wake up once or twice a night, and newborn baby Teddy was nursing with mom. At that point, we decided to divide and conquer: baby and mom over in right field, dad and two others over in left field. Or we would have gotten up about six+ times a night between all those kids. But, alas, my partner was still stuck in his old routine of hockey loving, fan clubbing, sport lover, evening fantasy stuff. Poor guy thought he could keep it all up.

Eventually, by the time Teddy was three months old, my husband's lack of sleep spun him into a sleep-deprived anxious state. He went three nights without sleep, which triggered extreme anxiety. That anxiety turned into such a deep fear of not being able to sleep that the cycle kept on repeating itself, which led to exhaustion, anxiety, depression, and a zombie partner and Dad. This was a lot to handle, given I was the stay-at-home parent and not getting a ton of sleep myself. We needed to be a team, and he just couldn't do it. We reached out for some help, got him on some light form of anti-anxiety meds to see if we could gently help him out of this state (a state which I had never seen in the twelve years we had been together—it was scary, to say the least). It all gradually evolved. Teddy started sleeping longer stretches, and the other two boys adjusted to a bigger family and grew out of wandering the house each night.

It has been two years since then, and my husband is still struck with anxiety and worry if he doesn't have a great sleep one or two nights in a row. All our children are finally in a better place and habit, thank fucking goodness! But for him, it will be a lifetime of consciously being aware that if he doesn't prioritize his ZZZZ's it is possible to snap into that state once more.

Are you prioritizing your sleep?

Here is what WE CAN DO: be more conscious about how much sleep we require. Again, I am no doctor, but I will share some of the things I have learned over the years of being a champion sleeper, due to my routine and consistency.

Know the tell-tale signs of tiredness for yourself and for your family. Develop a routine and stick with it. Your reward: every health benefit listed earlier. (If that's not enough for you, I don't know what is.) For example, I know that my perfect fall-asleep time is the window of 10:30-45, and if I hit it, magic. If I stretch that (and from time to time I stupidly do), I wake up at exactly 12:30 a.m. with restless legs and have to get up and go take something.

When I hit my magic sleep window my reward is an awesome day killing it: being a great parent, inspiring others, and having creative time. My routine is to get the kids to bed, create or write in my studio with a chamomile tea, head upstairs for a bath, brush and floss, get into the bath, say what I am grateful for out loud and breathe deeply, watch a show for thirty minutes while soaking, head to bed, read, hit the lights. No worry crosses my mind, because, number one, I am exhausted from killing it all day, and number two, I do this same routine nightly and my body and mind know it's time to go to sleep. My bedroom is my oasis. I get the softest sheets I can find and make sure that this feels like the greatest gift of all, to go to sleep. For me it really is; it is one of my favourite parts of the day, and I look forward to it.

List some ideas you might have to implement in a routine for your life. It may take a week or two to set in, but these activities or habits will quickly become part of your routine and you will no longer think about it.

List three things you could change about the habits you currently have.

1.
2.
3.

List three ways you could create a better sleeping environment.

1.
2.
3.

Here is what we use to create a great room for sleeping children and adults!

- A bedtime routine, like a bath, journaling, or reading to quiet your thoughts
- No light sources whatsoever (including night-lights)
- Blackout blinds
- Sound machine
- No using your phone in the bedroom
- Taking the TV out of your room (the adult bedroom is for two things and two things only: sleeping and bow chicka wow wow)

These items should all set you up for a better night's sleep—you're welcome. I will say it once, and I will say it again: ***sleep is your number one priority to living a happy, fulfilled life. TRUST ME! SLEEP IS PRIORITY NUMBER ONE!***

Routine & Consistency Are Key

Our very fit friend Chris once pointed out to me that having muscle literally burns energy/calories just while you are sitting there. Swallow that fun fact. "Lunges, Brandi, do as many lunges as you can, and you'll get legs like these," while he yanks up his shorts and flexes his massive pale thighs at me! I love really intense fitness people because they are always high on endorphins, and their energy is palpable! I mean, I will never be one, but I love them. I like being medium fit, thank you very much. Middle child, medium fitness, neutral like Switzerland, smushy but strong.

Being strong and feeling good is also very important to me, obvi—I'm writing a book about it. But really, why not get a few more of those endorphins flowing to help you out on a daily basis . . . couldn't hurt, right? OR, what about feeling the best you possibly can? OR, how about strutting into a room with the confidence of a child with a brand-new haircut and a lollipop? OR, how about maintaining that level of confidence with ease-ish? OR, feeling so good, you'll just want to keep going? SOLD! to the reader/listener in the back!

Now, the BIG secret is . . . nope, no diet around here. Routine and consistency are key. This can literally change your life. Health habits and routine. That's it. I do know someone who wrote a whole book about it, so if you are interested in diving in more it will change your friggin' life! Drumroll please . . . my favourite book about creating habits is *Badass Habits* by Jen Sincero—she likes cigarettes and fried food, so don't be intimidated. Jen has basically transformed my whole life with her books; I highly recommend ALL of them! She just released this one and it is my jam, a Jen jam, raspberry jam level, jam crack. It's good. Get it or listen to it.

Adults and children alike love routine; they know what to expect and when to expect it. Comfort and ease—what we naturally love in a day. Remember, anything you do to improve or throw into your life as part of a new routine you start with baby steps and soon it will become your consistency. Your brain will start including it naturally into your day as a habit, it will become easy, and you won't have to think about it all that much. What I am asking of you is to show up, open up, show up again, and show a whole lotta compassion and care for yourself.

For example, when I was eighteen I started drinking tea. I hadn't gotten into coffee, and I'd read in a magazine that tea was good for you, and I was into learning more about all the benefits (and there are a whole lot of them). At the time, it tasted like soggy socks soaked in water, and I was like, *Why did I buy this?* I had a Ted Lasso aversion to the stuff.

Now, at the age of thirty-five, I look forward to my tea regime (because I noticed that coffee made me twitch and crash): my morning green tea, afternoon black tea, and nightly chamomile. Like, really, honestly look forward to them; they are a huge treat. This is the perfect example of slowly integrating something nourishing into my life and how it has become a healthy habit, and then just a habit I don't even think about, and a habit I look forward to. I am not a doctor or expert by any means, and before you delve into some weird tea cleanse, look into what's best for you. This is just my experience. I also had a similar experience when it came to red wine, but that story doesn't end as well.

Another example of creating a healthy habit in my life is when I arrived at Red Deer College and my amazing Boston Marathoning Aunty Anna convinced me to join the cross-country running team. I was eighteen, with a bit of a chip on my shoulder and very into my social life (which included some social self-destructive drinking I don't feel like elaborating on by any means). Reluctantly, I showed up to the first running practice in the fall—my aunt is one of those people you can't say no to. What can I say? She has a gift; she could convince a person wearing a red shirt that it was actually blue.

So, there I stood with a bunch of young people I didn't know about to tackle 10 km together! The team headed out four times a week at 5 p.m. on different sets of trails throughout the city. Against all my hesitation and doubt about how I fit with this eccentric group of kids and the coach with the shortest shorts I had ever seen on an old man. Brian (said old man, who was probably not that old, just old to an eighteen-year-old) also confidently rocked a bike helmet from 1988; he was awesome, as you can gather from my description!

The experience was something that, A) I didn't think I could do, but my aunt saw something in me I didn't see in myself, and B) led me to the most fulfilling experiences and best memories I had in my college years. I was exposed to a different group of people and a healthy lifestyle that I integrated into my everyday life, which probably got me through many hormonal eighteen-year-old mental struggles. We took team trips to the mountains for amazing hikes to the summits—who knew I could climb a mountain, twice actually, and once in a freakish snowstorm, where I thought we would all die. We could only see 2 feet in front of our faces, but this seventy-six-year-old man led the way with his dog and I thought to myself, *He seems pretty leathered and seasoned from the outdoors, like he's done this before. Let's just follow his footprints in this deep snow and we should be fine. . . .* We eventually made it to the top and back down for the best spaghetti dinner I had ever eaten.

Being a part of that team exposed me to experiences I could have never imagined for myself. It pushed me out of my comfort zone and introduced me to new possibilities. I can't say that I would be the same person today had I not joined it. When my husband and I vacation now, we love hiking with our family. I run four times a week outside because I love how it makes me feel—nothing beats the fresh air and the endorphins to follow. It sure burned off some beans at the end of each day of student life and kept me out of trouble—for the most part.

I had a choice: Be a bum in my dorm or hit the trails. I chose to go outside of my comfort zone; I tried something new.

What about you? This doesn't have to be huge or complex; start small and integrate a new habit into your life, and in time you will be addicted to the health habits. Whether it be introducing meditation, running, walking, reading, being outside, just show up! Be compassionate to yourself and know that you are worth it!

Find a time of day that best suits you and find the activity that you most love doing. Those two points are key because you need to keep doing them. If you love them and if you find a time of day that works, then you are more likely to stick to it. As I said before, this is not a diet, but a lifestyle: routine and consistency are key. I know this works because I've done it, and I believe you can too! In that one little moment before making the choice to try something new, the decision could be the difference between resenting your everyday life or loving it!

Take Jenni for example. She wakes up at 5 a.m. every morning to hop on her bike and get whatever she needs to do done before her three kids get out of bed for school. Jenni also has an early bedtime routine and her wakeup time works for her because of that. She found her ideal time to take time for herself, even if it is early as fuck. You couldn't pay me to be a part of that club, but this is what works for Jenni and she loves it. She described it as a challenge at first but she started with using a gentle wake-time clock every morning. Before she knew it she was in a routine and now she doesn't have to think about it—it is just something that she does. She found what works for her. If she can do it, so can you!

If you are not active daily, I challenge you to wake up each morning and decide to do one of the following activities from your list for ten minutes. If you find that the morning just isn't for you, try your lunch break. After some time stretch it to fifteen minutes, then twenty, and so on and so forth.

List three activities you already enjoy doing:

1.
2.
3.

The Hardest Part Is Getting Dressed

While we are on the topic of getting dressed let's use working out as the example, or better yet, let's get specific: spin class, oh ya! Spin class is pretty badass, so a perfect example. Spin class: high energy, a lot of work, movement, endorphins, and sweat. It takes a lot of dedication and discipline to get to a regular spin class. But I can tell you from my personal experience that the hardest part is getting dressed (and that goes for any activity). Making the choice to do something that is good for you is something you need to do every day: move your body. Do we reeeealy *want* to go spin our brains out? No, we want to chill out, eat a bag of chips, dip them in ice cream, and stream Netflix. But if we do that, we will end up feeling like a trash can, and get in a toxic situation and a cycle of unhealthy habits.

But once those padded shorts are fitted to your bottom, it's on like Donkey Kong, bitch! You get there and are so pumped up, the music is dope, your blood and sweat are flowing, you are matching everyone's energy around you, and it's AMAZING! After the class you feel like you're on top of the world and you could do anything! AND like you should probably do this all the time because it FEELS SO GOOD, right?!! CHOOSING to not do the stuff that makes you feel like a trash can equal good stuff for the rest of your day, and the rest of your life.

But then, there you are two days later, contemplating another three episodes of *Schitt's Creek* and there is a bowl of cereal with your name on it. We live in a time in which the world can distract us at our fingertips, and everything is readily available at the drop of a hat. It is no longer about survival and owning a cow so you can milk it to feed your family through the winter season. We now have forty-one choices of milk at the grocery store. Your day is about what you choose and how you choose to live it. Are you going to make the best of it? Are you?

You know things are good for you and you know some things are not—you just need to learn how to integrate those good things into your everyday life and find a balance between them. You can be your best self for you and others if you choose to do so. It's a decision you need to make when you grace the world with your presence each morning. It takes dedication and passion and want, a want to live a fulfilled life because you know you deserve it. Start your day, put on or pack the outfit, book the class, hit the pavement or mat, whatever it is for you, get moving.

The task is to remember what makes you feel like a trash can and what doesn't! Let's figure this out.

What makes you feel good?

1.
2.
3.

What doesn't?

1.
2.
3.

Now, make the decision—make a commitment to feeling all the good feels for today and the rest of your days.

Kicking Your Own Ass into Gear

My most useful tools for sparking immediate joy and bringing you back into the present moment are: music, books, and movement. Get dressed and access your form of instant inspiration!

Music is such a huge one—what a gift it is! Think about it! We have the world, literally, at our fingertips. Every kind of musical expression can be accessed, and you can, at any time, let it flow freely through you. When I enter my art studio, this is my first move; it helps me show up, it feeds my needs, it fuels my creative drive, and it sparks magic! If the kids and I are in an afternoon funk, stuck inside, and the house is trashed, I use my mom's old move—I throw on some upbeat tunes and we dance and laugh and move our bodies together. They love it, I love it, and there are beautiful memories right there.

Books are a special tool in more ways than one. You can be transported to an imaginary universe someone else has created for you. They can evoke emotion with a single word or phrase. Now, for you non-reader types, audio books! I've seen people re-evaluate and make drastic, positive changes in their lives from a few inspirational audio books. How amazing is that?! The magic of the written word can be transformative! Audio books, for me, are a great way to dive into self-help every day. Physical books are a treat at night for me to escape into.

Movement . . . we were made to move, flow, age, change. The endorphins one can gain from movement in any form are marvellous. I love running or walking, in particular. I run angry, I run happily, I run to meditate. I walk to find peace, I walk with my kids, I walk to breathe, I walk to take in the world around me. Move alone, move together, move. Move fast or slow, just move.

Think about this for one moment. What kind of thing lights a fire under your ass!?

Great, now use what you know!

Nobody Cares

I am going to throw my partner under the bus here . . . sorry, dude! As a child, my husband and his sisters were avid young swimmers in a swim club. I don't think he ever was extremely passionate about swimming (anything your parents forced you to do as a child at 6 a.m. I think one would naturally hate). He does, however, love the fitness side of swimming and the perks that go along with it—he loves how it makes him feel, in terms of health and energy. But for years I asked him why he doesn't pop to the pool to fit in some lanes at lunch or in the morning. He has always answered in the same way: that he needs to be in better shape to go to the pool. This hang-up has held him back from something he enjoys doing. Many people suffer from the same syndrome: I need to be better or the best at something or the societal ideal before I can "dive in" or "take the plunge." You say to yourself, "I can't do that, I'm not good enough," or, "What will people think of me?" We always hear the same old "can't go to the gym, I am not fit enough, people will stare at me and judge me and think I look stupid or don't belong here," etc.

Stop it. Stop. Move past it. Why? Because this big, brave step will move you that much closer to the best version of yourself. In the same breath, the gym or a run or yoga (whatever you do to keep your body moving) will get you that much closer to where you want to be! Well, what I would like to say to you is: *fuck it, fuck them, this is about you!* Put your earbuds in, slap on some tunes to get you flowing, and throw on those tight pants. Don't move for them, move for you. Hit the trails like Phoebe in *Friends* without a care in the world. Get the endorphins flowing, feel good. Move in order to be the best person you can be for you, only you.

Let me just fill you in on a little something. People are typically too self-involved to even notice you. They are so caught up in what is going on in their world that they are more concerned about their own bodies, or thinking about what they have to get done at home, their next task at work, and so on. So rock on, let go, and do what you do—don't let anything hold you back.

What are your favourite ways to move your body?

1.
2.
3.

If you can't think of anything, Google some options, then close your eyes and visualize yourself in some of the environments where you can get moving. Or just start by moving at home.

There are so many ways to move at home if you are a little shy. Like really inexpensive ways, or expensive ways, running shoes, or no shoes and the floor, special bikes and neat machines, or apps! Not like us oldies over here. . . . When I was young, we didn't have the money to get any sort of equipment, so I would run up our staircase, go running outside, or just do my routine in the middle of the living room for all to see. Yes, my siblings made fun of me, and if we'd had smartphones back then, I would have been recorded several times over. But I didn't give a shit, because this made me feel good; it balanced out all the hormonal rage boiling inside of me. Now, I personally love just packing my runners and walking, hiking, or running wherever I am. Getting outside really impacts my mood for the rest of the day. I am a much happier person when I start my day off with fifteen to thirty minutes of movement and fresh air.

I remember reading somewhere that the later in the day you allow for working out, you are 80 percent less likely to do so. So get dressed right away in your workout clothes and then you just don't have a choice. After a while, this will become a habit and routine and you will begin to really love it. And remember, nobody cares!

The first thing you need is good ol' motivation, and that is all you will require to get moving.

Nobody cares! Here is the perfect example to reinforce the fact that NOBODY CARES (because they don't). My sister and I were chatting about how everyone is just so wrapped up in their own lives and she brought up this scene from one of our favourite Canadian shows, *Schitt's*

Creek and the episode "Driving Test." Two of the main characters who are siblings, brother and sister David and Alexis, are driving to a DMV so David can take his driver's test. When they get there, David is all stressed and freaked out over taking the test and Alexis says to him, "You are acting all kinds of crazy right now, it honestly does not matter, nobody cares." To which David replies, "I care. The driving examiner cares." To which Alexis replies, "No, he doesn't. Trust me, people aren't thinking about you the way you're thinking about you." David questions her and says, "What does that mean?" Alexis states, "You always overthink everything, and that's why you fail all the time, David." They proceed to argue and David explains to Alexis she skates through life and everything lands in her lap, to which she replies, "I don't skate through life, David. I walk through life in really nice shoes." She also tells him that "maybe if you could just relax for a second and stop worrying about everything, everything would be easier for you." She then leaves the car and says to David from the window, "David, nobody cares." The scene ends with the driving instructor worrying about his DJ gig and playing on his phone the whole drive, and David realizes that Alexis was right—nobody cares!

It's true. Everyone is so mixed up in their own shit piles of shit that they really don't give a hoot or holler what you are up to. You do you. And you do you with the best shoes on!

Love Yourself

"Love yourself and then life becomes a party."

– The Queen Badass Herself, Jen Sincero

Would you ever be as hard on a friend as you are on yourself? I'm going to take a wild guess and say no. But for some strange reason we feel the need to subject ourselves to these tortuous, unattainable standards. They are unattainable for a reason. In the beauty industry, for instance, they need you to keep consuming—return customers are their business. They keep pushing the bar and we keep buying in.

But these standards, not just beauty standards, but LIFE standards. Like, how many things can we be juggling all at once?! I need to be the perfect mom, while having an amazing career, perfect skin, and a skinny but curvy body? Have your kid in every sport on top of going to school, look and act like an adult with their shit together, cook three homemade, organic, vegan meals a day . . . shall I go on?! Unattainable, right? I do actually believe we can have some semblance of balance, but it has nothing to do with having it all. And it has everything to do with how much you accept yourself.

I remember the day I decided to love myself at every stage of my life. And I'm still working on it. I aim to keep on doing so every day. This is me. This is you. Fucking rock it! We are all human. We only have the capacity to take on so much in one day. All these things can overwhelm you and make you feel like you are constantly carrying this load of heavy water buckets, only to find that at the end of your journey those buckets are empty.

The way to carry all this is to not try to do it all in one day. Break it down and try to do a few small tasks here and there throughout the day. Giving it our all. Stopping when we need to stop. Creating a flow and natural consciousness of what we can handle and where we can fit it all in by finding our unique routine. When you practice self-awareness and notice emotions or feelings of overwhelm, take note and take pause. You can observe the times when you should rest or pause or work or move or play. Find those natural times and be aware where you thrive in each of these times.

The practice of loving yourself will allow you to set yourself up for success. Take note of when you are feeling your best and be conscious of how you are managing your time.

For example, if someone asks you to do something during a time when you are already overwhelmed or feeling low in the day, say "not now" and suggest a better time. Mornings are a great time for me to have my meetings or interactions. I am my best self when I am energized in the earlier hours of the day. About 3 p.m. I hit a wall and struggle to interact with humans.

Stop holding yourself to others' standards—you do you, sister sister! Be proud of who you are, and how you got here, and that you have the capacity to take on whatever life throws your way. Love yourself. Every little single bit.

Take Pause

There are just times when we need to take it easy. I want you to rest—you, us, we. We all need rest throughout the day. Not just a quick vacation (which, if you're anything like the stage we are in with small children, is an actual nightmare, my actual worst nightmare). In all aspects of our lives, we cannot be the best selves we need to be if our bodies are in a constant state of exhaustion and recovery, work, work, work, crash, work, work some more, get super-sick, crash. This is the BIGGEST task I will ask of you, why? Because it is the most commonly ignored. If you can't take care of yourself, how can you expect to take care of others?

Rest, too, comes in many forms: going to see a movie, ordering in, meditating, reading, walking, running, breathing, floating, hiking, a long bath, whatever floats your boat, drinking tea, sitting in the bathroom hiding from your children (men have done this for decades, it's our turn, dammit). There is this thing called burnout. I tend to hit it every once in a while; I just go go go, and there is never enough time in a day. Or I don't realize I'm burnt out and my body gets sick, which takes even longer to recover from. What should I have done in the first place? Realize that I should take a second to take care of myself, not just sporadically, but constantly throughout the day.

I have not done a ton of therapy, but the main point they always recommended for me and which I still use and practice daily: pause. I actually did therapy like ten years ago, and only this year did I start meditating and pausing. Let me tell you, this shit works, LIKE ACTUALLY WORKS! I don't want to brag or anything, but I will just a little bit. I am currently, right at this moment doing these things: being paid to create a university transfer course, starting an art academy for children in our public school system, doing a 135-foot mural, finishing this book, running a podcast, preparing for a solo art show in two months, runnin' my business, and momming full time. Proof! Right? Following your passion and taking care of yourself allows you to be the very best person you were meant to be! Yep, I need my breaks during the day. I meditate and hold Teddy tight for a snuggle once or twice a day. I work when they sleep—lucky my partner is hockey-obsessed, because he does that in the evening while I do my art thing! I love when I can hit two birds with one stone, multitasking motha motha!

Bringing it down a notch here. Take the conscious effort to pause. It's like a supercharger for your brain. It honestly feels like I am sharing my superpower here with you right now! But let me share with you how it could work: You just got the kids to school in a fury of house chaos, or you just sat down at your desk at work. You made yourself tea or coffee. Now, stay with me . . . you took time out of your life to make, pay for, or pick up said drink, correct? As time is our most precious commodity, are you going to sit there and chug that beverage in a fury if you have a meeting . . . the emails . . . oh, my phone just dinged . . . or there is shit all over the floor . . . NO! You are going to sit with that fancy-ass, best-part-of-your-morning drink and savour every sip! Pause. Notice how it smells, how it feels on your lips, what it is like swishing through your mouth. You are going to breathe, look around, speak to someone face to face. Is there anything around you that you didn't notice before? You get where I am going with this, right? Give your body and your mind a chance, open it up, and be grateful and soak it all in! Bring a respectful level of consciousness to your day and continue to do so several times a day.

Integrating acts of pausing into different areas of your life will allow you to find a counterbalance to the highs and lows. A great example of this is recording when you feel low in a day. Note the times and how you feel at each time. For me, in the morning, I like to pause to eat and drink tea when the kids are gone and read something inspiring and make notes. Right before I make dinner in the evening, I close my eyes and snuggle with the kids while they chill (a quick fifteen to meditate or sometimes nap). At night I take a pause in the bath: with a gratitude list. In bed and with a book. It is a glorious routine that quiets my overactive mind.

Recharge a few times a day to find your balance by taking pause.

Are there a few times a day you could take five to ten minutes to pause?

Whipped
cream
and
Sprinkles

Whipped Cream & Sprinkles!

The Power of Positive Reinforcement

Throughout university I was taken aside countless times by my professors about my inability to write an essay. They were concerned because they could tell I did the research and the work—it was the execution that lacked.

I wanted to write an essay, I really did, I just could not compute. I just didn't get it; I wasn't there yet. I wasn't interested as much in it because it wasn't a strength, so it was ignored. I was continuously told that I "could not" in a negative way. Until my last year of university, when I enrolled in a History of Hitchcock course. I signed up because I thought, *Amazing, we just sit and watch films all semester, SCORE!* Which was pretty much what we did, but then we had to break them down and learn all about filmmaking. I was hooked. I fell in love with film and the whole creative process. Our professor had graded my papers on scene breakdown highly—this had never happened to me, exams and essays not my jam, but this felt good. Then came our final paper. . . .

For the essay we had two months to choose our topic from the given themes. I was one of the two students out of fifty who chose to write about the aesthetics of murder in the writings of Edgar Allen Poe,

Thomas De Quincey, and Oscar Wilde and how they impacted Hitchcock's filmmaking. It was fascinating, to say the least. As a person who can dive into other creative minds and let it take hold of their own mind and soul, I was invested like never before. My professor had been encouraging and was excited about my topic choice. I worked harder than I ever had, and in the end got an A+. I know it wasn't an A+ paper I had written, but I had worked that hard, he could tell, and he graded accordingly. It was that positive feedback and encouragement that sparked something inside me. It was a lesson that, if I was interested, and if I set my mind to something and worked hard enough, I could figure out anything. I had been told I couldn't and proved I could. All I needed was the slightest amount of encouragement and someone who believed in me.

Now I have taken it upon myself to impact the lives of the youth in my community to have someone to believe in them. I guess if you say your community needs an art academy enough times, someone calls you about launching an art academy. I am happy to announce that I will be now working in our public school system doing just that. Encouraging kids to discover their creative interests, as well as positively impacting their lives by developing a curriculum that encourages them to pursue their passions and apply those passions to their chosen studies or careers.

Here I am, thirty-four or thirty-five years old (one of those), writing to you, with bells on, happy to be here, and I hope you are too! Teddy, my youngest of the three boys, is two now, and I am encountering the time where I might have to join the workforce once again. The thing is, I want to—I did seven solid years of stay-at-home parenting, raising three very busy boys and keeping my art career afloat while doing so. It was a crazy journey, but I am ready to put on my big-person pants and leave my house. I'm soooooo ready. I mean, I made enough to pay for groceries while staying home (which we all know cost a fuck load), so I am pretty proud of that. Because full-time parenthood is not easy, and throwing a career on top of that was the ultimate challenge. But I really, really, really love what I do—it's all I talk about, and that is what makes it worth it. Stick me in a room with a piano and I will write you a song. Lock me in a closet with a paper, pen, and flashlight, and I will write you a book. Lock me in my house with my kids with an art studio, and I will paint 300 paintings (that happened, by the way). I live to create, no matter the outcome.

But somehow, along the way of parenting and trying all these things, I was impacting others. Inspiring by example, and making people think, *Hmmm, if that crazy, goofy woman who is at home raising her three kids can pursue her passion, maybe I can too.* And you can! *Hmmm, if that artist is making a living from her art, maybe I can too.* And so on and so forth.

Here is your permission slip:

You are capable and strong. You can accomplish whatever you set your mind to. You will fail, and you will get back up again. You will succeed, and you will celebrate every accomplishment. You will love what you do. You will love the people you choose to surround yourself with. You will wake up each and every day happy to be you. You will wake up each day and relish in being alive, because you are worth it.

Work It!

I didn't grow up with a lot of money. We always had a roof over our heads and food that warmed our bellies and just enough to get by—that is all we needed; it's really all anyone needs. We had love, and with that we had enough and more.

By the time I needed to go to university, though, there was no savings or any sort of money for schooling, and apart from student loans, or what

I did in the summer months to earn enough money to get by, pay rent, and pay for groceries, it was always just enough—not any more, not any less. It's funny, I hate numbers and have never loved money, but I have always figured out ways to have it. I would finish each year of university with about $11 the day before going home and starting my summer job. Always just enough.

I think it's called a good internal clock maybe? You might know. I'm going to go off point here, but here's a nice example: As I mentioned earlier, when I was at Red Deer College I was on their cross-country running team. Every year, Brian—the one with the short shorts and the helmet from the '80s (got to love Brian!)—our eccentric, dedicated coach, would throw a fall race called "The Turkey Trot." And whoever guessed their race time for the 5k run and ran the race closest to the guessed time won a turkey. It was so fun and weird and everyone was there for a good time. I love running communities; you just find the most supportive, amazing people, and in Red Deer there is such a great one. Anyhoo, the first year I ran in Brian's Turkey Trot I was seven seconds off my guessed time: hands-down win. A fluke, you say? I think NOT! The following Turkey Trot I finished with a record-setting guessed time of four SECONDS OFF! Four is my lucky number, so naturally I would finish off my time on the cross-country running team as the ultimate Turkey Trot Champion (this is not actually a thing, but I certainly like to think it is)—my plaque still hangs on the wall, thank you very much. I can't think of a better way to describe my perfectly tied internal clock to you, but it is ticking away in sync with every step of my day! Some call it luck, some call it intuition, some call it god, some call it the universe. Whatever it is, it exists.

Okay, back on track here . . . I paid my way through school doing a number of things, one of which included selling shots of alcohol out of a bucket (and I am not ashamed in the least). Now, this wasn't exactly what it sounds like. Yes, I did sell shots to large groups of (mostly) gentlemen, BUT I was in no way selling myself, and I never felt like I was sacrificing a piece of myself or was unsafe in any way. I looked at it as a learning opportunity, one in which I was gaining experience in social skills which I still use today. I was capitalizing on an opportunity and was a master conversationalist who needed at least $10,000 in two months! It was the only watering hole for a 200 km radius, and it was hopping, packed full of hundreds of patrons each night. It was the peak of our economy and people were throwing out money and I was catching it (suckers). To call it the happening place was an understatement. IT WAS THE ONLY PLACE! It was packed with everyone from oilfield workers and members of the Canadian Army base to firefighter trainees and every hot-blooded young person in our city and its surrounding counties.

I was young and probably would have attended said club regardless, and I really needed some cash for school, so win-win. To my great advantage, I chose to reap the benefits of having the urge to party as a young adult, and being somewhat financially on top of things. I still got to have a social life, minus the costs associated with that lifestyle. Not to say I didn't sample my share of the Kool-Aid from time to time. However, like most things in life, I had my own unique way of approaching things. There were fellow employees who pursued the route of flirtation—I innately knew this was not in my repertoire per se, as I was terrible at it and always ended up embarrassing myself in some way. Upon first glance, many have made that assumption (as most people have) with me: oh, she is just a pretty girl with not much to say or offer.

Without flirtation on the table, I took the approach of friendliness and being one of the gang! This was my hometown after all. Anyone I didn't recognize was surely a mere tavern visitor. My go-to was, "Hey, everyone, where are you all from?" Not even offering them a drink, just a simple friendly conversation. I would stroll out of there with money stuffed in every sock, undergarment, and boot because I couldn't fit it onto the money fan I held in my hand. I made that $10,000 in two months selling shots two nights a week! It was absolutely nuts, and a ton of money for me at that time (shit, it still is)! It was a lot of fun and filled up my social cup—two birds, I always say! The only downfall was being up until 3 a.m., but I was young and had energy and made it work! I worked hard and applied myself, focused on what I needed for the goals I had set for myself to have money to live across the country and attend university to ultimately pursue my true passion: art.

Upon graduating with my bachelor of fine arts degree in my last year of uni, I thought to myself, *Great, no more scraping by and working until 3 a.m. Surely a career awaits just behind that graduation door.* To my utter dismay and disappointment, that was not the case, and the very week I arrived home my mom said, "Okay, you can live here with me, but go get yourself a job TODAY." Fortunately enough, we live in a place where getting a same-day job is possible, and that's just what I did!

After a lot of moaning and groaning about having already waitressed for six years, I reluctantly headed out the door of my mom's condo. The first place I went was the newest restaurant in town at the time, a local Greek place called Spiro's. I walked in to meet Maria, the part-owner/manager and daughter of Spiro himself. She hired me on the spot. I think I had a pretty border on my paper resume (this dates me, if Blockbuster hasn't already), and she said, "Wow, no wonder this is so beautiful—you're an artist. I've never seen a resume this nice." Although, I am sure it was laced with grammatical errors and flaws, she saw the uniqueness and was willing to take a chance on me, albeit not that big. My dad being a chef, I had a lifetime of experience in the industry and six years of hard serving leading up to that. At the peak of the economy, they would hire just about anyone who was willing. The most wonderful surprise at my new place of employment was that Maria, my new manager and I connected immediately and I looked forward to seeing my new friend every morning. I will be forever grateful for the opportunity she gave me that day, and so many others. I am proud to still call her my friend. Present day, I just finished a figurative custom artwork of Maria for her bathroom—she is a stunning human.

To be honest, at the time I was still very young and I had a lot to learn about work ethic in general. I was disappointed that having a degree got me absolutely nothing except a few nice paintings that I sold for not very much money because I couldn't afford to ship them home. (Side note: those people are laughing now, because the $50 painting they bought from me is now worth $10,000 + in value. Hopefully they held onto them—if that's not a sound investment I don't know what is.)

Back at work with a degree, and not much to show for it, serving once again, I was majorly bummed out. For about a year I didn't put a lot of effort into serving because I really didn't want to be there. I had an "I am too good for this" mentality. It was just a job, and I needed the money to pay off my $40,000 student loan debt. I know so many of you have been in this exact same boat, or still are—I feel you, friend! Let me tell you, though, the "I am too good for this" attitude never works out in your favour—it just makes you a dick.

I am getting to a solution for you, and something that changed my ability to turn a job I took for granted into one of the biggest sets of building blocks that added to the foundation of where I am today.

I'll Say It Again: The Hardest Part Is Getting Dressed

Whether you are working from home, working out, meeting a client, getting your work boots on, or putting on your uniform, the hardest part is ALWAYS getting dressed. At least these days, if we are working from home, we have the option of keeping on our comfy pants, am I right?! I loved all those videos of newscasters getting up with their undies in the middle of a live broadcast. Got to celebrate those little perks and great blooper videos.

Getting dressed is always the biggest struggle—just move past it as quickly as you can and rip off that Band-Aid. Dive into the icy cold water . . . you'll adjust in a minute. Once you are in the middle of whatever it is you are inclined to groan about, it's really not so bad. In fact, when it comes to working out, I always put on my clothes first thing in the morning so that I cross it off right away. And as soon as I am moving my body, I start to have fun, my mood lifts, and I begin to enjoy myself, and this gray cloud floats away from over my head, the sun breaking through the clouds of my day.

Looking good, feeling good! I always say that to my sons when they throw on their clothes, and nine times out of ten I get a big smile from them and I can see a little brave pep in their step. Put on your best of the best and go for it! Say it in the mirror, *Looking good, feeling good!* You will be ready to take on anything!

Don't Just Get Dressed, Put on Your Costume & Play the Part!

For that first year I coasted by at my job back in my hometown, where I had once vowed I would never live again. It was a long year and I resented being there. I felt like a failure because I didn't immediately do something in the arts after I graduated. What was it all for I wondered? Being half-depressed and reading the Twilight series and discussing it on the side with the owner's thirteen-year-old daughter Zoey . . . a bit of a low for me, I must admit. "Is Edward really going to leave Bella, tell me, is he coming back?" Soooo low.

Imagine me there in the back of Spiro's kitchen: adult braces and hair short from a bad buzzed haircut, the result of a miscommunication in

Thailand (another story, another time) . . . looking back, this was a very humbling year for me. I would simply wet down my bedhead, put on my black uniform, and go off to work. This same routine day in and day out of the not-all-there me wasn't working. I wasn't happy, and it hurt in so many ways, but I didn't have a ton of options at the time. You know, the loan debt, no car, and the whole living with my mom situation . . . I would show up barely presentable, just on time, and move through the motions of the job. No one took me seriously, because I wasn't taking myself seriously. I would get yelled at for being a nincompoop, some customers sucked to serve and I let them know, I would complain about it and them, to a point where I couldn't stand even myself, but yet kept trudging through the mud with my head down, complaining to anyone who would listen. The pathetic part is that I had been in this industry my whole life—as I mentioned, my dad was a chef and I was a complete natural at it. It was my attitude and perspective that was causing me to shit the bed.

Until one day, when I finally caught on to the opportunity that was staring me right in the face for a year: you can be better at this if we just look at it in a different way. I finally started to notice that the seasoned servers in my workplace were making some mad skrill, at this same job that I had been coasting along in and doing alright. But at the end of the day, I didn't have a lot to show for it other than just paying my bills on time, and I lived with my mom, so what bills am I even talking about here? A cell phone bill and a minimum loan payment, monthly.

I'm not sure when or exactly how this all shifted, but it did, and thank goodness for that! I started wearing fun jewelry, cool scarves, things that set me apart and made me feel good in my uniform. My hair had finally grown back a bit (which helped with my confidence), and I got to at least attempt to have a hairdo. I still had braces but was never afraid to laugh or smile, because when I dressed for the part, it made me feel better, more confident. Except for the day I had spinach from the spanakopita I ate leftover from the lunch buffet stuck in my front teeth . . . good times.

I showed up thirty minutes early for my shifts and stayed the latest, because if you closed the restaurant you always got the big tables. I was pleasant to staff and customers, even if I didn't really "feel" like it that day. I showed up with bells on, and always in a consistent and professional manner. And ya know what? Even though I often didn't feel like going, within the first hour of my shift I was having a genuine good time! I said to myself, *By gosh, if I am here, I am going to be the best server in this tiny Greek restaurant!* AND LOOK AT THAT! I WAS a master at it. I could memorize a table of twenty-five by the end of it all (this was still in the paper-and-pen age, kids). I was a wiz and when it came to upselling and I was rolling in it!

During this time, I became close with this beautiful family that started their business from scratch and fought tooth and nail to do well through economic downfalls, bankruptcy, and staffing issues—they found a way through it all. They were the most intelligent, resilient people I had ever met. Spiro would sit with me after my shift and we would chat over red wine in a tumbler glass. They cared about me and shared their wisdom of how to get by in the world. They had immigrated from Greece years ago and are still moving and shaking it at their extremely successful family business. Tina, Spiro's wife, just started her own cooking show called *Yiamas with Yiayia*—so cool, and Maria's daughter Elenee is now taking their business to new levels. I supported them, and they supported me and we continue to do so. We are still close to this day, and I am grateful for all the lessons they taught me in those years and the support they offered even though I was an ass some of the time; they let it go.

In that year that I decided to show up dressed for the part I paid off my student loan debt and had a shoebox overflowing with Canadian bills, y'all. And if you don't know, in this country our smallest bill is a fiver. No singles in that box!

What you can take away from my experience is this: people can feel your energy; they bounce it back at you. AND it is so obvious that in the hospitality profession it benefits you greatly and monetarily to be likable—that is true of any industry, for that matter. This all should have been a no-brainer from the start, but hey, we all live and we all learn.

A Little Bit of Suck

No matter what path I decide to take in my career, every profession comes along with a bit (or a lot) of suck. You really have to decide what job you don't mind doing the unenjoyable parts of. Musicians need to perform at night when the average person likes to make dinner and wind down from their day. But they are passionate about creating through sound and that is their compromise. But there are parts of their industry, like production or song writing, that they could do alternatively if they didn't like the evening performances. This isn't cut-and-dried for any industry, not so black-and-white—you can find a little wiggle room. It is about learning to embrace the suck as long as you get to do what you love.

My Dad is retired now from being a professional chef. He worked his ass off, twelve- to sixteen-hour days and not a ton of pay. He had restaurants go bankrupt, and he wasn't around to see us when we were young as much as he wanted to be. I actually found one of my mom's holiday letters that she sent out in 1989. My Dad wasn't even there enough to get into the photo—my mom cut out and photocopied him in. Gosh this letter makes me laugh; I miss my mom so much.

Dear Friends & Family:

Well 1989 has been quite a year for us.

We've been pretty busy. Rob opened up another Restaurant. He's been occupied with that (as you can tell from the family picture!

We had a little time at the lake this summer and also took a trip to Calgary. I spend most of my days with the kids, helping out occassionaly at the restaurant (the pay is lousy!).

Zachary has finally made it to grade one! He is still playing hockey and enjoying it. He also won biggest fish this year, beating out his mother! He spends most of the day hoarding his toys from his sisters whom he affectionately refers to as "Swamp Thing" and "Sister Lizard"!

Brandi turned three in July and has mellowed considerably. She even enjoys going to Church contrary to her sister who probably won't see the inside of a Church for another year or two!

Kayley has really grown and she will be two in March. She spends most of her time defending herself and has taken up biting and hair pulling as her premiere methods! I have visions of her and Brandi forming their own rock group (Screamin' Sisters), as they practice, oh, about 25 or 30 times a day.

MERRY CHRISTMAS from all of us to all of you!!

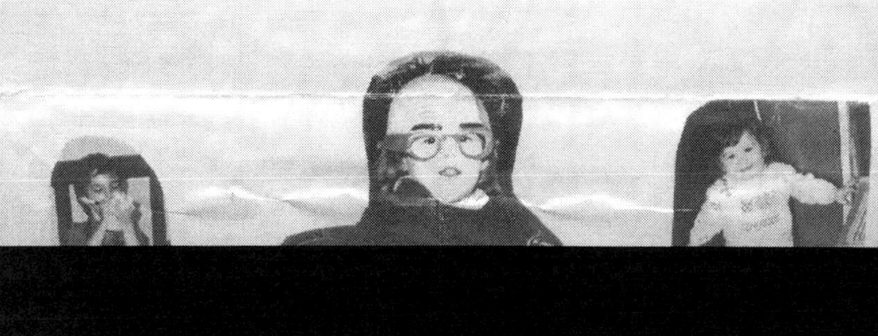

I know that he loves being a grandpa to my three boys because it's his chance to redo fatherhood, and it is a gift. I was talking to my dad's mom, my grandma, on the phone last week, and she was telling me how much he is enjoying helping me and that it gives him real joy and purpose.

I have to tell you this story because it is just the perfect example of what my days are like right now with three boys ages six and under. In that very phone conversation with my grandma I was in the basement for twenty minutes; Teddy napped and Finn was having "quiet time" in the garage. I kept hearing the pitter-patter of frantic steps above my head. My grandma is sick and eighty-nine years old, so I didn't want to cut our conversation short. Finally, I said, "You know, Grandma, I really need to go. I feel like I'm about to walk into something up there." Lo and behold, Finn had taken six bottles of soda (I don't even know from where, because we don't drink pop), one pound of sugar, and all of baby Teddy's pureed fruit packs and poured them into five baking bowls on the garage floor—sticky shit for days!

The next day the boys had a friend over, and when his dad came to pick him up I told him the story about Finn. He said, "Just one of those days." I replied, "Nope, that is my every day." We laughed. But just to prove themselves, the boys decided to really, really make a point of being stinkers that very evening—it's like they said, "Yep, mom, we accept your challenge, and we will do you one better," followed by maniacal laughter (MWAHAHAHA). Friend and Dad leave, and I notice that all my tampon boxes are lying on the floor empty. Where are all the tampons? Where are the sixty-four TAMPONS? Teddy likes to flush the toilet, great, soooo they are gone. Yep, the toilet IS clogged. Okay, I will go get the plunger. Walk over to get that, then notice that Teddy has pulled out the alarm and the cords are pulled out of the plug and the alarm is beeping and driving me bonkers. This will take an electrician to fix, but naturally I called their dad, thinking, *I can fix this by stripping a few wires myself.* He said to forget about it, but I don't; I try to fix it, forgetting all about the clogged toilet. Then I hear Finn. "Mom, I pooped." What? No, no, no. Gah. Ah, hold on, let me grab that plunger again. Teddy walks over and flushes and flushes and flushes. I don't really have to tell you what happens next. . . . Point proven, guys—you are so busy that not one person can keep it all together.

At this point, I have become a bit numb to all of this and am no longer surprised or thrown off by it all. I'm done with all the guilt that comes after yelling, and I don't want to be that kind of person.

Again, back to the saying from the Indigo Girls: *You just have to laugh at yourself because you'll cry your eyes out if you didn't.*

No matter what it is, staying at home, pursuing a career, a part-time job, no one has it made in the shade with a glass of lemonade. All days come with a little bit of suck in them. You just have to choose what kind of suck you don't mind on a daily.

Make a Plan

When you are in a job that bites the big one, you hate it, it is sucking the soul and life right out of you, and you groan when you rise out of bed in the morning, cursing the lords. Or, perhaps you are in a job you know wasn't really meant for you, but maybe it will help propel you to the next big step. I mean, you got there somehow, so there should be a way out of it or beyond it.

I am going to help you out here: make a plan. If you HAVE to be where you are, do it well, and find the fun. Get dressed. Play the part. Embrace the SUCK. People and opportunities will gravitate toward your energy; it may not happen tomorrow, but it will happen for you one day soon. Visualize it, write it down, make a vision board, create, and say your mantra (we will go over this more soon). Do whatever you can, when you can, to the very best of your ability. The experience of being in the fast-paced world of hospitality was a stepping stone, a building block for me, preparing me for the larger things that were coming in my life, and I still utilize that skill set to this day. Use whatever situation you are currently in to get to where you want to be. You have choices and the ability to do so.

You will turn your "have-to" into "I *get* to," and attract the life you've envisioned for yourself. All will come when you shift your mindset. If you adapt the mentality of, *I get to*, people will gravitate toward your energy; it will flow around you, and you can lead others down the same path with your positive example and ability to move forward, adapt, and create the beautiful journey you've set out for yourself. Say what you want, shout it out loud, or at least just say it out loud, every day—say it, sing it, write it, rap it. You do you; just let the universe know. Tell people your plans, because you are more likely to do something and follow through if everyone around you knows and will hold you accountable. I've been probably 25 percent more driven to finish this book because I told everyone I would. I am incapable of keeping secrets, and I fucking told everyone over a year ago (it might be almost two now) that I was writing a book. Fuck. Like EVERYONE else, I was so excited. I was thirty pages in at that point. Oh boy, little did I know how much time and effort and people it took to make a book happen! Knee-deep, all in, here we go! If you're reading this, I suppose I did it after all . . . happy dance for me, and thanks for being here, new friend.

The following are some big questions. Take the time to think about your answers—you'll be surprised at how constructive these questions are, and you should revisit them yearly.

What is your current employment situation?

Would you like to be there? If not, how is it applicable to what you would like out of life?

What are some things holding you back?

Where would you like to be in a year?

Where do you see yourself in five years?

I Get To!

This is the practice I like to call: *I GET TO*. When you wake up, the first thing you have to do is take into account what you *get* to do, not what you have to do. It is simply changing the words. Being grateful through subtraction. Simply put: you didn't realize how important your right thumb was until you lost it. My mom's friend once went snowboarding for the first time and broke both her wrists and was in two arm casts for months. I bet she was damn thankful when she got the use of her hands back! Could you imagine? Just think . . . how can you wipe your butt? Enough said. I *GET* TO HAVE HANDS.

"I get to's." Your "I get to" will be a lot different than mine, but I am going to share mine with you so you can come onto my plain for a minute:

> I get to get out of my comfortable, safe bed that has soft sheets and the best pillow of all time. I get to be woken up by my happy, sweet baby and nurse him quietly before dawn, and before the world wakes up. I get to be alone in my thoughts with my baby's tiny, chubby hands holding my cheek and he pauses to say, "I lalu too, mama." "I get to" moments are the most precious. I get to step out of my bed with my healthy body and get to put on my running outfit and shoes and run my strong muscles and feel the fresh air on my face and feel exhilarated the whole time, taking in the peace and beauty of the world. I get to make breakfast for my special little family with the food we can pay for in our fridge and get them off to the school that is close enough to walk to. I get to spend time with my tiny baby alone, because while funds are tight, we made it work for me to be able to play the role of a stay-at-home parent. I get to go into my

studio and have the freedom and ability to create and write and connect with and support creatives and people from all over the globe. I get to greet my children after school when they walk home to our safe neighbourhood and play with other kids while I make dinner. I get to read books and hear about all my children's thoughts and dreams in their safe beds. I get to spend time with my husband and partner, take a warm bath, read, and go to sleep.

When you think about your "I get to's," life becomes a cup that is half full! This just really makes you ponder: What do I already have? What do I have to lose? What is important to me?

In my podcast *Colour Me Happy!* I have the final question called *a day in the life* sponsored by my kick-ass GF Jill from Red Bicycle Communications (an all-female firm that she started from scratch, so proud of her). Okay, so I have this awesome final question in my pod. I have it because I am genuinely so itching to hear everyone's answers. I get them to describe their ideal perfect day. The answers are simple and all very similar. For the most part, they describe a quite slow day spent with their families. I fully agree, and this is proof that when you strip everything away these are our deepest desires: to be happy and healthy and to spend time with the people we hold dear, period.

Start at the beginning of your day and list your "I get to's" below:

-
-
-
-
-
-

Building Blocks

One thing will always lead to the other, every stumble, every fall, leading you, preparing you for what is to come next.

Although it took me a year or two to get over the fact that I didn't walk into an art-related job after graduating from university and was back in hospitality, there were a great number of things to take away from being part of that industry for so many years. I would not give this time back, because it was all a part of the process of building a solid foundation of building blocks that led me to where I am today. I acquired an over-the-top work ethic. Learned to be a lot more social, as well as the importance of being well-spoken and polite, approachable, likable, clean, and disciplined. The most valuable of skills I learned was being organized and efficient and becoming a master multitasker. I still use these skills and carry them forward into who I am as a business owner, entrepreneur, and parent. Without the skills I learned in that type of industry I wouldn't thrive at what I do today, nor would I appreciate the fact that I now have the opportunity to be my own boss and pursue my passion. And how one thing always leads to the other in the most magical and unexpected of ways.

In 2018 I was approached by two women who founded our local women's conference. They asked me to be one of the speakers to lead off the event early in the day. This would require me to write and recite a fifteen-minute speech in front of 300 people. Being that I had zero experience speaking publicly, I was reluctant to say yes. In grade nine I cried in front of my peers reading aloud my poetry . . . since that moment, and for good reason, I had avoided any situation or setting where all eyes were on me. However, I also don't like to say no. In fact, I have to learn to say no more, which is a whole 'nother bag of beans.

When I was asked to meet up with those two amazing women who ran the women's conference I agreed to go for coffee with them only because I liked them—I hadn't actually planned on saying yes to speaking, like, in no way; this is just not really something I did. Like I said, since that mortifying poetry moment in middle school I had avoided public speaking like the plague. At the meeting their excitement and encouragement was contagious. They gave me the confidence that I could do this and that I could just talk about myself a little. *Alright,* I thought, *I can surely find something compelling to tell 300 women IN PERSON, ON A STAGE, WITH A MICROPHONE.* Now, I knew that this actually wasn't something that came naturally to me (and it was before we all started making stories on our phones) and that I needed to work on it with the most vigour I could muster. I poured two months into that fifteen-minute presentation on stage, because:

a) I had never done anything like it before
b) I had no idea what to expect
c) I had no idea where it was going to lead and what I was doing it for

All I know is that it scared me. I didn't know exactly what I was going to say. But I sat down and got started. You know what? It was one of the most touching and empowering paths I have ever travelled down, and it has led me to many, many more beautiful opportunities. I said yes because, again, someone saw something in me that I hadn't seen yet, and even though I didn't see it, I got there, surprised myself, and really blew away everyone in that room. As it turns out, at the event I somehow pulled it off! It was an amazing experience, one that I will never forget, and now I've opened a door to so many more opportunities because of it, including this book and other speaking engagements. I had a taste of how my creativity can be a beautiful gift that inspires others. In fact, the presentation touched so many women that I still get messages all the time. They even had me back to speak in a more intimate setting. It is one of those intense moments that you cannot describe in words. That experience led to me having the confidence and belief in myself to be writing this book, and touching your life today. So don't overthink it—embrace an opportunity, even if it scares the pants off you. I promise it won't be so bad in the end, just fifteen uncomfortable minutes of your whole life. Remember, everything in your life is a building block, preparing you for what is to come next.

Don't Overthink It!

At that Woman's Day event they had one of those cool pop star singer mics that attaches to your head, and the first thing that came out of my mouth onstage was, "Wow, I feel like Britney." It was game on from there!

This speech was one of the most terrifying and fulfilling moments I have ever experienced. Here I was with this incredible opportunity to touch 300 other women's hearts and minds all at once. I was there to connect and fill them up, move them, and come before them stripped bare.

I had the opportunity to give a similar motivational speech again online to 400 + more women, and I don't know how this is possible, but I could feel us collectively weeping together through our computers, as one.

What you choose to do with your abilities can move people. You have it within you to change and inspire others, and lead through example. Those are the things that really matter. How are you going to leave this world a better place than when you arrived? You find something you are passionate about and share it with the world. That's how. The rest will figure itself out. You won't fail. Every day you will get out of bed happy that you are here. Because you are doing something you love.

That speech was titled "Don't Overthink It." It turns out I did have a story to tell, and it went a little something like this:

> *As I was putting this project together the title was the first thing that came to me. It came, along with a memory, a not so good memory. Something another art professional said to me once a long time ago. They said something along the lines of, "Do you just like to do things, and not think them through beforehand?" They were not being kind, and definitely meant it as somewhat of an insult. Being caught off guard, the only way I could respond was, "Ya, I guess so." Up until this presentation, this conversation and encounter has always annoyingly hung in my memory as an unpleasant experience, and something that someone not so nice said to me. But I am here today to tell you a small version of my life story and how not "thinking things through" just may have led to the most beautiful and rich experiences that I have had in this life and this is where it began. . . .*
>
> *When I was part of another artist's project that was set in Montreal titled "The only thing I know for sure, is while I'm looking for you, you are looking for me," there were two people chosen to participate in the project, and they were to set out in the city and find one another within thirty days. As a part of the requirements to apply, you were unable to know anyone in Montreal beforehand. The other individual was someone who I did not know and who did not know me. We didn't know what the other looked like, if they were a man or woman, their age, nothing. AND we were not allowed to use the internet as a resource to find one another.*
>
> *The third day I was there I got a bike from a young man named Andrew, whom I had met swimming in a fountain one evening.*

I had never actually ridden a road bike before, nor had I biked in a large city. But for some reason unknown to me, I was welcomed into Andrew's road bike posse immediately, and within minutes, we were weaving in and out of Montreal rush-hour traffic. I was scared and terrified, but completely exhilarated! Every day after that, I covered at least 40 km on that bike through Montreal. I encountered special events like group yoga, electric dance parties, salsa lessons, and the Tam-Tams. I ended up being interviewed on CBC twice and having a live painting exhibition at a gallery to promote the project. I didn't find the other person in Montreal, but I didn't view that as a failure, because that experience was life-changing for me. I was pushed beyond every expectation I had of myself. I was surprised at how I thrived independently in a place that I was unfamiliar with. It was an extraordinary time of growth for me. I learned to be independent. It had never really occurred to me until that year that I could do anything on my own, eat dinner, go to the movies, and live alone for thirty days straight. I didn't need anyone to take me where I wanted to go. I had finally discovered that my life was in my own hands. That was a very powerful moment for me.

Two months later I was to travel to Marnay-sur-Seine in France for another artist's residency. I met some stunning creative minds, from all corners of the globe, and began hearing all of their stories while I painted them. The residency was set in the countryside 40 km outside of Paris. I got pleasantly plump and glowing from the fall sun, warm baguettes, soft ripened cheeses, and flowing red wine. It was completely picturesque. Almost every day, I would get on my bike and ride down a country road in the orange sunlight passing fields of sunflowers. The old brick residency was right on the Seine. Trees sagged beautifully over the waterway. It was how everyone should experience France.

In that period of my life when I was in my young twenties I said yes to everything without thinking, and embraced the unknown. In my thirties, in amongst the darkest periods of my life after I lost my mother, I somehow found the light. Through troubling and hard times, I chose resilience. I have given to this life and life has gifted back a wonderful childhood, a loving family, stunning life experiences, and the most sensitive partner and loving children.

And I have chosen to take something negative, something that someone said to me, that they viewed as a flaw, and turned it into one of the most beautiful things about myself. Without my bravery and inability to "think things through," I could never have come to realize my capacity for creativity, found my unique view of the world, and found an insurmountable lust for life.

What I am bringing forward today, to you, is, do you have the courage to find bravery within you? Do you have the courage to live life moment by moment? Find something within you, something you never knew you had. We don't know what is to come; there is no control over time in this life, so, with every ounce you have, squeeze and savor every moment. And "don't overthink it," because you may just end up missing out on something magical.

Now, I want to finish with this story about my mother: Some months ago, as I was searching through old photographs and some letters my mom left for me, there was this page torn out from a notebook, along with something she had written along the bottom. As I looked closer, I discovered that the page had been torn from a comment book from an art competition I had entered years ago. I had placed first in the competition and someone left an unsavoury remark on how they disagreed with my receiving first place. My mother had saved it for over ten years, and when she was sick, she left this for me to find with a note at the bottom. She wrote:

Dismiss with love all those who don't see beauty in the world

- love mom

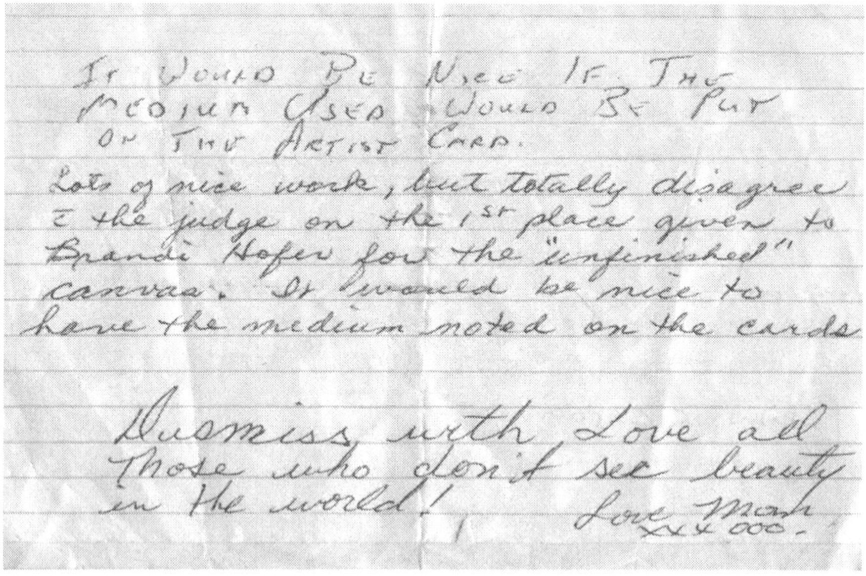

IT WOULD BE NICE IF THE MEDIUM USED WOULD BE PUT ON THE ARTIST CARD.
Lots of nice work, but totally disagree c̄ the judge on the 1st place given to Brandi Hofer for the "unfinished" canvas. It would be nice to have the medium noted on the cards

Dismiss with Love all those who don't see beauty in the world! Love Mom xxx ooo -

Just Be You, No Exceptions or Takebacks

I will never forget one of the most well-known movie scenes from *Wayne's World* in the car where they sang Queen's "Bohemian Rhapsody." EPIC. Did you know that Mike Myers insisted on that song, in particular, in that scene? He told the producers he wouldn't do the film if they refused to use that song; they, however, thought it too big a risk. He wanted it to be the exact way it was when he and his brothers and their friends listened to the song in their car when they were teens. He literally put a multi-million-dollar foot down and risked it all for his artistic vision. Mike knew—he creatively visualized the scene and its magic, it was part of the integrity of the film, there was no other way—and lo and behold he was right! That song was one of the most epic songs of ALL TIME, that scene was epic, and it skyrocketed both the film and the song's success.

Speaking of Queen. When you think about them, do you instantly think of Freddie Mercury? You think of him not only because he was the lead singer (after all, the lead singer is usually the one who sticks out in every band), but also because he was unique. He, daresay, refused to be ordinary (aside from a great internal struggle). He could not hide or disguise his passion and the way he expressed himself through music and performance. People could feel his energy and his passion. Their band was a band of misfits that created a spectacular magic no one could quite put their finger on or ignore. They were so successful because they stood up for their creative vision, even though people told them it wouldn't work. It worked because it was special, and everyone could feel it, because each and every one of us is special and it ignited everyone who heard it.

Be you, be the honest you! There is no one like you, nor will there ever be another. The power to live your best life comes from within you. Get down with your weird self! And remember, dismiss with love all those who don't see beauty in the world, dismiss with love all those who don't see the beauty in you.

For example, if your daily job is sucking the life right out of you and you absolutely hate it. The best way to look at it is to think of another job you could do, or how this one could lead to another opportunity within or past it.

What are your interests?

What is your natural talent? And is it something you could do for a living, or start to do and eventually quit your full-time gig?

Overcoming Fear

> *"Fear is going to be a player in your life, but you get to decide how much. You can spend your whole life imagining ghosts, worrying about the pathway to the future. But all there will ever be is what's happening here in the decisions we make in this moment, which are based in either love or fear."*[3]
>
> – Jim Carrey

In life, there are pros and cons and a reaction to every action—striking balance—a spectacular and harsh reality. Which reminds me of the first summer I spent with my partner, now husband, when I crashed their "boys" trip to Jasper. Really, there was no separating two people newly in love. I was twenty, he was twenty-two and we were newly punch-drunk in love and high on life—such an exciting time. One of our activities on the trip was mountain biking to a spot called Horseshoe

---

[3] Jim Carrey, transcript of commencement speech delivered at the Maharishi University of Management, May 30, 2014, https://www.rev.com/blog/transcripts/jim-carrey-commencement-speech-transcript-2014-at-maharishi-university-of-management.

Lake, where you can cliff dive. When we arrived, I was exhilarated. Thinking about it, this was probably the first big destination I had travelled to where one of my parents was not in attendance or I wasn't with fifty kids on a school trip (proud band geek over here). The sun was shining, people were swimming and laughing, and we were having the time of our lives!

We popped a seat on the rocks below and watched people climbing to the top of the cliff and jumping off. I think it was about 80 feet high. After about thirty minutes or so I thought, *Yup, I'm going to do that, yup, yes, I am fun, and crazy, and yes, yes, I can!* We trekked up to the top. I recall my heart pounding out of my chest—even writing about it makes me breath heavily at the memory; my pulse increases just in recalling this exhilarating experience, a moment I will never forget because my body is physically reactive to it.

Once arriving at the top we paused just briefly, about 20 feet from the jumping-off point at the top. In the fifteen minutes it had taken us to climb to the area near the cliff edge where people were jumping off, the same young man we saw from below was still stuck at the top and standing on the platform—he was frozen in fear. It had overtaken him, disabled him fully, paralyzed him. I knew then that if I looked even once over that edge the fear could take hold of me as well. I thought to myself, *No way, I am not about to take that chance. I am alive, I am a woman, I am brave!* I yelled from where we stood, "HEY, YOU, move over!!!" And I ran off.

Plummeting 80 feet into ice-cold water at an angle: Ouch! Fun, but ouch! Pros and cons. Pro: it's a very cool story, and I will always remember how exhilarating and how amazing life is. Con: I will also remember how my tailbone was bruised for months afterward . . . totally worth it though. It's funny, maybe I wouldn't have jumped if I hadn't witnessed the other young man frozen, refusing to plummet. Would I have jumped if he had not been there? Would I have been also stuck on that edge?

The moral of this story is, move forward, take one step in the right direction each and every day, and jump—or you might be paralyzed forever on the cliff edge. Take that young man, for example. Visually see him not jumping. Life is just like that. When we let the cons outweigh the living, we get frozen in fear. Don't overthink it.

You may have a few bumps and bruises along the way, but don't let it stop you from leaping. Make memories, take risks, live, for all we have is right now.

Jumping off, for me, was an unforgettable, amazing memory, a memory of a bright, exciting time in my life of what it was like to fall in love and what it was like to be young. It was made even more special that I got to share this memory with the person I chose to marry and start a beautiful family with.

Think of a scenario where you let fear hold you back.

Now, how does that make you feel?

What is the worst thing that could have happened if you had done said scenario?

Now, what is the best?

If You Are Your Own Disbeliever

That tiny, mean monster pops in every now and then to say: Who are you? Why do you think you could write a book or make the world's tallest cake or be your own boss or become an avocado farmer? What will everyone think? What will they all say? What if you give this speech and cry or freeze? What if you make a painting and no one buys it?

If that was an issue for me, I would have not created any paintings at all. This has actually happened to me quite a lot, and it's never stopped me from painting a day in my life. Sometimes you have to do things because you want to, and when it comes to painting, it's one of those things I do not because I want to, I just HAVE to. It is a part of me, woven in every depth of my being, and it comes out in every word I speak or write.

But yes, I, too, have all those terrifying thoughts that sneak in through the cracks, and they are very real fears. I have become hyper-aware of when they decide to pop their ugly heads in. I notice it mostly late at night or if I am having a particularly tough day because the baby was up too many times the night before, when I am so mentally exhausted I just can't handle much more—that's when I start to doubt myself and my journey. What I have learned, and am still learning, is that I have to allow myself space to rest and recharge. Stop working, stop trying. Slow it all down, and do some of the things I enjoy. And not try to balance motherhood and the work and the house and carry the world on my shoulders. Focus on the moment right now that I am in control of. Quiet my mind, breathe, and keep a mental check on my self-talk:

You are doing the best you can; beyond that, the rest is out of your control. Okay, now all I can handle is getting the kids to bed and to take a bath and do some light reading. We will try again tomorrow.

What happens is when I do take the time to rest and recharge, I wake up restored and with all the gusto I can muster and start the day with my personal mantra: *my creativity is worthy and powerful*! What is this life to you if you can't *PUT A LITTLE MUSTARD ON IT?* (If you haven't found a mantra yet, you can borrow this one for now!) I am proud of myself that I have the bravery to welcome in my passions, my desires, and this creative urge to do something I have never ever done before. Listening to your gut is kind of scary and exhilarating all at once, and it is kind of one of the big reasons we are who we are. You should do things that scare you; they will move you forward, and they will mould and shape you into the beautiful person you are, and the person you were meant to be. They will take you to unexpected places and exhilarating heights.

You must first believe in yourself, and the only way to get comfortable doing all the other stuff is to tell fear to step aside and just dive in. The water may be cold and you may not come out unscathed, but what a thrill it was and will be! The more you do something, the less scary and intimidating it will seem. It will become monotonous, a blip on your ever-expanding radar and repertoire.

While doing all this, remember that you can do anything, but in the same breath, you can't do it all. A good place to start, though, is at the beginning. You've got this!

Challenge yourself. Embrace change. I know it's scary and it's the monster that lives in the unknown depths of your dark basement, where all your fears linger, but it is also very exciting. Take it from me, the most exciting things that have happened to me were absolutely terrifying at first! And I always questioned what the heck

am I doing? What on earth did I get myself into now? However, overall, I can say to you with complete resolve that all of those things were unequivocally worth it!

Is there anything in your life that you've wanted to try but were too afraid to do?

The Trick to Getting Anything Done

I love how Elizabeth Gilbert describes passion in her book *Big Magic*. You treat your passion like an affair:

> *"Stop treating your creativity like it's a tired old unhappy marriage (a grind, a drag) and start regarding it with the fresh eyes of a passionate lover. Even if you have only fifteen minutes a day in a stairwell alone with your creativity, take it.*
>
> *Go hide in that stairwell and make out with your art! (You can get a lot of making out done in fifteen minutes, as any furtive teenager can tell you.)*
>
> *Sneak off and have an affair with your most creative self. Lie to everyone about where you're actually going on your lunch break. Pretend you're traveling on a business trip when secretly you're retreating in order to paint, or to write poetry, or to draw up the plans for your future organic mushroom farm.*
>
> *Conceal it from your family and friends, whatever it is you're up to. Slip away from everyone else at the party and go off to dance alone with your ideas in the dark.*

Wake yourself up in the middle of the night in order to be alone with your inspiration, while nobody is watching. You don't need that sleep right now; you can give it up.

What else are you willing to give up in order to be alone with your beloved?

Don't think of it all as burdensome; think of it all as sexy."[4]

How different would the world look if people thought their jobs were sexy because they were pursuing a career in something they loved? What if they were happy, passionate and excited, lusting for life? I would say that we would have a lot of huge issues in our society resolved. Because in this exploration of pursuing your passion you will find yourself. In your pursuit of passion, you will be taken on life's greatest adventure.

In writing this book, I will tell you how it came to fruition and I just couldn't stop—the ideas, the words were swirling through my mind and onto the page. Yes, this is what Elizabeth refers to as BIG MAGIC, and there is no other way to describe it—and boy is it fun! I highly recommend time for love, passion, and exploration. Who knows where it will lead (isn't this exciting)?

The coolest and most rewarding part of my journey is when I teach people or take on a mentee and they again connect to that part of themselves. They describe it to me exactly like above. It's all they think about, all day, they can't wait until they have the next opening to work on their newfound passion.

"The subject matter of art is life, life as it actually is: but the function of art is to make life better."

– Gertrude Stein

---

[4] Elizabeth Gilbert, *Big Magic* (New York: Penguin Random House, 2015), 161.

I have an abundance of personal experience and proof in magic. It is sneaky and sly; it reveals its face at unpredictable times. Though I know it is there, always lurking, waiting to crawl up my spine and remind me that life is a special gift in itself. I want to tell you a little tiny secret . . . I love my magic so much that I don't wait for it to strike. I love my magic so much that I greet it daily with openness. I love my magic so much that even when I am doubtful it will appear, I show up. I love my magic so much that I nurture it and rest to restore it. I am forever grateful to this gift of creative energy that I behold and wish to spread and share it to others in all its forms.

Can you see it? Can you feel it? It is there, waiting . . . magic is within you. Open yourself to receiving it, whatever its form.

Throw a bunch of Spaghetti at a wall and see what STICKS!

Throw a Bunch of Spaghetti at a Wall & See What Sticks!

Find Your Passion, Find Yourself

Kate McKinnon, who many of you probably know from *Saturday Night Live*, talks about her life story in this Netflix special called *Breakfast, Lunch & Dinner:*

> *"You know in 6th grade there was this like school dance and they tried to get me up on stage, and I couldn't do it. I made a scene where I actually screamed. The following year at a bat mitzvah I figured out that if I danced in a funny way I felt free to do whatever I wanted and people would laugh. That's what feels comfortable for me."*[5]

She is so in love with what she does that everyone can feel it, the world can feel it. She is so passionate about what she does and has excelled at it. There was no other option; she discovered her thirst for

[5] *Breakfast, Lunch & Dinner*, Season 1, episode 4, "Phnom Penh with Kate McKinnon," aired October 23, 2019 on Netflix, https://www.netflix.com/watch/81076570.

laughter early on. And I have no doubt that doing what she does, day in and day out, takes copious amounts of dedication and talent that can only be fuelled by pure passion.

Be Inspired by Finding Your Productive Routine

Actively search for opportunities for inspiration: listen to music, make playlists, find a podcast of interest to you, read books—or listen to books if you are like my husband. My stubborn husband (who argues that I am the more stubborn one—to be fair, I am), who totes around the same two books that sit on his night shelf, and has been guilty of hauling those same books on every vacation he has been on for the last ten years, because surely he will learn to love reading magically, out of nowhere, on this upcoming vacation, only to haul the same two books home, taking up that precious space in his carryon. You need to find something YOU will STICK TO, and you need to find a routine that will work for you.

Read or listen to books if that's what you're into; if not, find the thing that gets your heart pumping. It can motivate you on the most tired and frustrating days and take you out of any funk. The funny thing is that people think that magic pops up out of nowhere, and that artists are filled with it, and magically they create masterpieces with all of their magic sparks. Kind of . . . but not really! All day I open my eyes to the beauty of the world all around me. I pause and hold space for it to fill me up. It is a routine of mental work and dedication to my passion.

My creativity is triggered like clockwork almost every night I hit the studio, pretty much no matter what, same time, and everything that has been filling me up can be channelled. Why does it work out for me, you ask? Because for years I have been consistently doing this same routine: kids to bed, make a tea, bring it down to my studio, headphones, music, work, create, feed my soul, and—most of the time—MAGIC! The funny thing about this is if I am out doing something at night other than being in my studio, around 8 p.m. I start hearing and humming my favourite songs. It is so amazing that because I have habitually started this routine for my practice now my body and mind expects it, longs to create, yearns for magic to flow out of my veins and onto the canvas or into the written word.

I can guarantee that if you introduce a regular and positive routine into your life your body and mind will come to expect and appreciate it.

Visualize, draw, or write something you'd love to incorporate into your every day and help your creative routine and make it a habit.

Focus & Energy

Where your focus goes, your energy flows! Opportunity and the life you want exists all around you—it's all about what you choose to see and focus on. Jen Sincero writes about visualization in her book *You Are a Badass at Making Money: Master the Mindset of Wealth*. She writes:

> *"Once when I had a hankering for a tuna fish sandwich, I went to the pantry to grab a can and found my craving crushed under the realization that I was tunaless. The little blue can of albacore was nowhere to be found (insert sad trombone sound here). Right before I left the pantry in defeat, I thought to myself, I KNOW I have some damn tuna, so I kept looking and suddenly, lo and behold, right in front of my face there appeared two cans of tuna. The thing is, the cans were red, not the usual blue (I switched brands, you see), and because I was looking for blue, not red, I did not see them. I'm sharing this lunchtime suspense thriller with you because it illustrates how often we miss out on the golden financial opportunities, life-changing connections, and heart-opening experience that we crave because we're stuck in old ways of thinking, believing and hence, focusing."*[6]

Sometimes we can be so distracted by life and the drama and the emotions that we can't see the good things that are staring us right in our freaking faces! But what if we consciously noticed and took note of where we can steer our energy and how we can use it in the most productive manner? What if we could direct all our negative, positive, and emotional

---

[6] Jen Sincero, *You Are a Badass at Making Money* (New York: Penguin Random House, 2017), 128–9.

energy and blast it out like rainbow magic into the life we see for ourselves?! Wouldn't that be something?

Think about a situation where you could have saved some of your energy and used it in a different, more productive way.

Work Smart, Not Hard

After two years of being a mole in my basement, shifting my art practice and finding out what could work for me as a creative and what wouldn't, I will share the shorter version of the outcome of this story. I learned that for me, it's not just one thing that works. I can't just make paintings and have them sell and that is enough to live off of. It works for some, I know, just hasn't worked for me. And I gave it a good ol' fifteen-year shot. I am still going to make paintings. That I will never stop—I have three exhibitions this year alone. However, for the life I envision for myself and my family, and how I want to change the world through creativity and all that, I knew I had to take some really BIG new leaps.

In parts of my research and coaching and mastermind groups, other artists shared their money-making pies. In those pies some were doing murals. I had already done one 50x14-foot mural as my very first project (pretty nuts, but that's how I roll). I just wanted to give it a try, and turns out, it wasn't easy. The materials were uber-expensive, and it took me three times as long as I thought it would. But I didn't give up. No, I took that as my lesson of what I could change and tweak and make work the next time. I kept applying for mural jobs and poured thousands of dollars into videos, photography, and marketing, knowing that my pie could look like others in my field.

I can say now that I've since done ten more murals, and I just received a mural job for 135x20 feet—my largest project to date! Combining mural work and education, this increased my annual income by 394 percent.

Yes, it takes years and research and dedication, but if you can see it, if you put your mind and heart to it, you do the meditation, you put yourself out there, you direct all your energy into the life you envision for yourself, I believe YOU CAN DO THIS!

Close your eyes, take five minutes, and imagine the life you choose for yourself.

Get Support

When the pandemic hit initially, I met with an art consultant. She reviewed my website and all my social media platforms, and she asked what I was looking for as an artist, and what my goals were (basically). I had spent the last few years diligently creating bodies of work and collections in my studio, as well as taking on custom jobs. I worked my ass off night after night while my babies slept, creating artwork and applying to galleries. I spent three months applying and applying and not hearing back. This is normal for artists. Galleries take 50 percent of the final sale, on average. Nothing against galleries—they work very hard. This plan just wasn't working out for me. The art world, and the world in general, just aren't a formula you can follow. Everyone has their own unique journey.

My art consultant suggested I set up a custom artwork option straight from my site and run an art shop from brandhofer.ca, selling limited prints and originals as well. She said, "The world is quickly changing; let's give this a shot!" I agreed. It sounded cool, and obviously with years of trying the other path with no financial outcome, at that point I was game for anything!

Well, there I was, just under a year later: I had painted over 100 custom artworks and countless originals and produced specialty print releases, hosted my own solo show, and it was all a fuck-load of work. WOW. Holy shit, we had done it! I made double what I did the year before . . . awesome, but holy moly, that was a ton, a ton, a ton of work. After a good amount of reflection and evaluation and conversations with fellow artists, we came to the conclusion that this route was not so sustainable. Cool, people love my art—I cannot tell you how rewarding and incredible that feels! FINALLY, I had done it. But I sacrificed a lot of my time, and I was so, so, so, burnt out! Like I mentioned earlier, I barely had any net profit year after a year of painting my heart out.

This DEFINITELY called for a new way to express myself . . . keep some of the methods from the year previous, but what else? Hmmm. It hit me: why not a book, maybe education?! What the heck am I going to write a book about or teach people? Oh, well, I'll figure it out, maybe. I don't know. Then came holiday season burnout, thirty custom paintings later, just before the 25th of December (a bit of insanity, to say the least) . . . time for a massage! Halfway through my glorious bit of self-care I stopped the masseuse. "This may sound super weird, but I need to make a voice memo before this idea flies out of this room!"

It hit me like a ton of magic creative bricks: my title for my book and the amazing and huge realization that I have had this book inside me for years! Every blog post, Instagram narrative, tips video, motivational speech, and artist statement has led up to this point!! I AM going to write a book and capture on video some of my creative knowledge and share it with the world!!! I mean, I wake up with an insane number of questions and emails every morning asking about what I do and how I do it—this seemed like it should have all occurred to me a lot sooner than it did.

After that massage, I got home to my husband and his mother at my house and announced, "I FINALLY know what I'm going to write my book about!" They looked at me as if they had seen a ghost. Had I not told them that I was thinking about writing a book? I guess I hadn't . . . my bad. That statement was followed by a few "what the fuck?" looks and "are you sure you have time?" comments: "I mean, you kind of have your hands full . . . remember how you are a full-time parent at home already trying to maintain your art career?" They definitely took a beat to catch up—a week or two, actually. But the beautiful part of this is that they did catch up. They soaked in my enthusiasm, they encouraged me. They saw that this ambitious, crazy idea and plan lit me up from the inside out. It was all I could talk about! They hopped right on board! Why? Because they love me. They love me for all that I am. They believe in me, and they accept all the parts of me. I only wish that everyone can find support of that degree in their lives. You deserve love, and you deserve acceptance, in all of your forms.

There Is a Lid for Every Pot

It is lovely friends and beautiful people who lift you up and encourage you to go beyond what you have even imagined for yourself. I have been fortunate enough to have a supportive community with many creative friends, and we all support and encourage one another and are proud of one another's victories. The impact of community has altered my life in so many positive ways, it is difficult to express my gratitude in words to you on this page. All I can tell you is this: surround yourself with these people who will love you and support you. Together you will all do great things, beyond even what you see in yourself today.

How do you find these people, you ask? Let's get you a lid for your pot!

Well first, you must make a list (lists are my favourite, as you already know).

Describe yourself: interests, activities you enjoy, beliefs, pastimes, age, sex, occupations you are in or aspire to be a part of.

Take your description of yourself or your future self and start joining communities, mastermind groups, clubs, and pages. Follow, message, ask around. Don't be shy! We actually have this crazy thing called the internet and social media, and get this: it has a literal algorithm to find your friends for you! Easy peasy lemon squeezy!

This is of the utmost importance, finding your besties, mentors, coaches, community. Your environment can be so detrimental to your mood, energy, and the way you go about your day. If you are in an unhealthy relationship or friendship, it might hurt for a day or a month or a year, but don't let it hurt you for your whole life.

This is your opportunity to create lifelong friendships that will hold for you endless love, empathy, and support. You need community. You deserve love.

Some Seasons Are Meant to Strengthen Us

My lovely friend Ekaterina Popova (who is an artist, founder of *Create! Magazine*, *Create!* podcast, and the Art Queens, a coach, writer, and so many other things—be sure to check this amazing human out!) wisely said to me once, "Some seasons are meant to strengthen us." This resonated with me deeply—at the time I felt the burden of heavy burnout and was floundering—that no matter where you are in your journey, it is where you were meant to be. There is a reason you are here; it is just one of the building blocks setting up the foundation of where you were always meant to be.

After struggling for years to find where I fit in the art world as a young female Creative, I had finally found the oasis in my desert. Having a sense of community and support has changed my perspective. It has shifted the limitations that were heavy on my shoulders. Being a part of The Art Queens Society gives me confidence, strength, and a sense of community. It allows me to let go of any expectation or judgement. Being a Queen means finding women who are working as one, arm in arm, to change the world. My heart is full, and I am proud to wear the label "Queen."

It has inspired me to start my own community: "Colour Me Happy Community." It is full of wonderful creatives and tiny artists alike. Having this community has been one of the most beautiful adventures I've ever been on. A place where it is safe to be you and express yourself. You are welcome to join, friend.

Delegating

Do you hate cleaning? Me too. (I just assumed you would, but if you don't, I am so happy for you!) In fact, I was ashamed when I hired a cleaner. I worked full time, had my first baby, picked up groceries, made every meal from scratch, and painted in the evenings. I was EMBARRASSED to hire a cleaner to come every week. WTF?! Trying to do it all and be a superhero is just exhausting and not fun for anyone. Delegate and have no shame! I have someone else that scrubs my toilets and showers, big effing deal! Now I have more time to hang with my kids, and work in my art studio—or, I don't know, let's get real crazy, have a seat and take in the beautiful world around me!! If I don't have you convinced by now, riddle me this: if I'm not using my time to clean, and instead work in my art studio, ta-da, there are the funds. Trust me, delegate tasks you loath; it will make more space, leave you with more energy, and you will find a way to afford it. Less time for cleaning pee (I live with four boys, so this is my harsh reality), more time for fun!

This follows up with me finally getting a bit of help in my art business. I wished I could have an assistant. What would that even look like? Could I trust someone to that level? I really could use a hand with my banking. Was there anyone in my small city who could even fathom what the art world looks like? Can they pick up on what I have been working on for over fifteen years? This is scary . . . better to avoid it, right?!

And here is where the universe speaks: I call my sister and am explaining to her all my big plans and how much I could use an assistant, but it's hard to find the right fit for my particular business (especially in a very small rural city). She said to take Jenni; she would be so honoured. Jenni was/is my sister's manager for her yoga studio, which at that moment was temporarily closed for safety during the pandemic. Jenni, yes, Jenni, I know her (*Elf* reference)! She knows me, she knows my family and a bit about what I'm all about. If she can get along with my sister on a daily basis then we will be a great fit—nothing against my sister, but she lets few people in her trust circle, so if Jenni made it into the circle, she wins for personality of the year (or ten).

I'm no wizard with finances—not a terrible mess, just no Harry at the books! Jenni has sorted and organized—I didn't even realize the areas I needed assistance with—and now it's freeing up time and space for so much more. Now I can do more, achieve more, breathe, and make plans for the future with confidence, knowing I am no longer on this huge ever-encompassing journey alone. It feels so good! Since I hired Jenni, I have worked with countless others, handing out tasks where I don't thrive. I didn't have the money at first, but I booked the help anyway. I trusted myself to make enough to pay my new friends! Yes, I call them friends, because they are. When my business grew, I found the right-fitting people to help me.

The first step was joining communities in my field of work. I met others who were succeeding and reached out to them and they were happy to help. The worst thing anyone can say to you is no, but they can't say anything if you never ask. These people were not only integral to me visualizing what my art practice could look like, but they also helped me find services and ways to get where I wanted to be.

What is something you could delegate in your life?

Jealousy Is Not a Bad Word

I recently had an awesome coffee date with my bestselling author friend Jeff Hilderman. We talked for hours, but it felt like minutes. Sometimes we don't know our neighbours, but Jeff happens to be one of mine.

Rewind to two summers ago when I found out Jeff had written his own book. I heard about Jeff's bestselling author status from our other neighbours in our crescent who had read an article in our local paper celebrating his successes. There I stood, perplexed and—what was this feeling—jealous on this sunny day in my shorts and tank top, sporting my flip-flops on the asphalt. Let me see that paper . . . yup, that is not some other Jeff. That is a picture of our neighbour Jeff, hands-down. I thought to myself:

Huh . . . I had no idea he was a writer. What do you know, Jeff, who runs Home Hardware with his wife and her family, is a writer . . . a writer . . . a good one . . . a successful one . . . just featured in Forbes. *He lives right over there . . . remember, Brandi, being a writer is out of our league.*

Remember? Everyone told you; you were crap at it. But Jeff, a real-life person that we know, wrote a book . . . interesting.

I was taken aback, to be honest, and why was I jealous? I was a painter after all; that was the choice of career and I was deep in it, in the midst of parenthood and being a painter. Why was I jealous of Jeff writing a book? Being a painter was plastered all over my identity, not only by myself but others, and it felt at the time like I wasn't allowed to be anything else.

I now know that jealousy is not a bad word. In fact, jealousy is telling. It allowed me to realize that a book is something that was always inside of me, always trying to come out, but all the encounters and discouragements pushed it back down. Until it built and built and came up to greet me when I was ready, when I was strong enough to say, *I can*, and knew that I was goddamn capable of anything I set my mind to!

Fast-forward to the next summer, and Teddy, my baby, is striding by Jeff's house on his push bike and Jeff starts chatting to me, hearing that three months earlier I had decided to write my book and announced it somewhere on social media. Jeff, who hadn't said a lot to me in the five years since we all built in this neighbourhood. He had caught wind of my book secret and was excited to talk to someone who was tackling something he was so passionate about. We just kept talking, while Teddy zipped around up and down, up and down on his little red Strider. Jeff was full of ideas, and he lit up when he spoke about his process and all the people he met and the courses and groups he was a part of. It inspired me to hear more about his process and accomplishments. He wasn't competitive or above it all, which surprised me; he was invigorated and excited to share his experiences with me. He actually gave me the best tip I needed at the time (because we both have three little ones and are equally as busy): "Don't try to write in chunks of hours; try for ten to fifteen minutes every day."

That was the best damn advice. Ten to fifteen minutes seems manageable in my day, and I got it. Finding little tidbits of inspiration along the way and running to my computer to get them in before they disappeared. All those little bundles of time added up to, you guessed it, what you are reading right now!

Back to this very moment following my coffee chat with Jeff. This is the last thing I wrote in my book. Why? Because that last meeting over tea is what I needed to say goodbye (if anyone listens to my podcast you will know I have a bit of a hard time saying those last departing words). I need to take the brave step and get these words out into the world. What did I need? Apparently, one last tea with my neighbour Jeff. Friends do come from the most surprising places.

You need to befriend like-minded individuals, the friends in your world who are interested in similar things. Because they will take you where you need to go. They aren't your competition—they are your advocates. They lift you up and help you see something in front of you that you did not see on your own. Had I not had a pang of jealousy for Jeff's success, it never would have led to me taking on a book. Surely if my neighbour could do it, why couldn't I? Jeff was a real person who did something I thought was an imaginary venture for extraordinary people. Jeff was real. I saw him, I lived near him. He was a full-time parent and a business owner, and he found a way. By golly, if Jeff can do it, so can I! AND by golly if I can do it, so can YOU!

What are your dreams, the ones you think are out of grasp for you? List three below. Then try to find a good example for each dream of the people who have done it already and figure out how they did it. Now, find a coach in this same area—they can take you the extra mile!

-
-
-

The Secret to Success Is . . .

Jeff did let me in on his little gem with the fifteen-minutes-a-day tip, no doubt. The funny thing is I have already been doing this. I have NO choice—I have children; I multitask the shit out of my day. They need water, they need lunch, they need to go outside . . . I have to find all the little times and windows I can go create, work, or write in my studio. To be honest, I don't mind the breaks where we play outside or have a picnic. It's nice. It provides balance.

The key to an extraordinary life is to be present in many, many of those extraordinary moments that all add up to the extraordinary day. It is not just a BIG thing but an accumulation of many tiny things. The moments that are building blocks adding up to the tremendous tower of who we are. If at any given time you don't feel like you are achieving anything, or aren't hitting "where you think you should be," just keep in mind that it is not about the end results or the goals—that, my friend, is the killer of happiness. Know that where you are here, right now, is where you were meant to be, and to achieve any level of moving forward is to keep at said thing every single day and remain consistent. The most interesting and effective book I have read and would recommend to you on creating and maintaining habits is *Atomic Habits* written by James Clear. It is wildly popular!

Think about it. You didn't always know how to read. Eventually you cracked the code, and now reading is not something you have to work hard at—it is just something you do. This goes for anything. We are always learning and evolving. But when we are not seeing the results and aren't instantly gratified we give up. I used to get overwhelmed when I had my first home and got all the groceries; I would think, *Check, done for the day!* Now groceries, and cooking every meal, being with my kids, and all the other many things that are a part of my day, are things I just do and don't think about; they are just all a part of my life and my routine.

If you can't do something, keep doing it until you can, keep on until the can doesn't faze you. Again, these are all building blocks leading to something larger. This mindset can be applied to anything in your life. It may be overwhelming at first, but it is just one block in a tower of many, and you will add bit by bit to your tower: it is ever amassing!

Here's another example for you. I used to get extreme anxiety about emailing (stemming from anxiety I held on to from the years I was told that I could not write). I avoided emailing my audience and collectors at all costs. As a lot of us know, a good newsletter and mailing list are key to the success of a business. For ten years I avoided it. My list started with 200 people a few years ago and I have constantly emailed and posted and podcasted and interviewed and done motivational speaking, etc., and now I reach over 375,000 people a month through marketing. How about those apples?

The most common thing people say to me is, "I just don't know how you do it." The secret to my success is this: utilizing all the fifteen-minute windows in a day. That's it. My husband bathes my baby, I head down and write in my book. Thirty minutes before bed I go paint. Twenty-minute *Paw Patrol* window, I make dinner and so on. It's not me working at one thing for six hours straight. Those days are long gone for me. When so much needs to be accomplished in one day, the secret is all laid out here for you in this book: don't take any time for granted.

The Power of Visualization & Planning

When my parents separated when I was in my early teens my dad eventually acquired land outside of our city. He got this old house on 10 acres. Of course, my mean-girl teenage mind was like, *Ugh, why can't my dad be "normal?" What does he see in this place?* He then proceeded to pay to extend the dugout into this 200-foot pond/river thing. *Dad, why would you want to make this gross, ugly mosquito-infested dugout even bigger?*

Fast-forward twenty years later: We pull into my dad's drive (now Grandpa). My three little guys hop out of my minivan with an enthusiasm that can't be expressed in words. They run into Grandpa's arms, and we head into the yard, where peacocks, ducks, and chickens roam freely. The boys run through the garden and pluck an apple from the lush trees. They hop on the golf cart with Grandpa and go to the lookout tower overlooking the beautiful, giant pond where wild geese and ducks glide through the water. Birds are chirping and a peaceful breeze blows through the quiet oasis and the sunsets stretch for miles, the reflection orange and gleaming on the calm water.

Maybe you don't see it, but someone else might. My dad knew what he wanted, and he worked long and hard to achieve it. And guess what? I try my darndest to get out there with my children whenever I can. It is peaceful and it fills my soul. Hashtag life goals.

What are the top five things that are important to you?

1.
2.
3.
4.
5.

Where do you see yourself in ten years?

Lists!

I love, love, love lists, if you haven't caught on already. When you have a list you get to gloriously cross things off of it—oh baby, it feels so good!

Put them on your phone, write them on paper, write them on your ceiling, your wall, on a Post-it, take a voice note, write it on a napkin at the bar . . . I do not care! You will have the great satisfaction of writing a list and then getting to cross it off—oh sweet bliss!

Making lists is a great way to quiet your thoughts and organize your anxieties. Make lists for your day, week, and year. What is neat about this is that you can come back to your agenda or notebook and see where you were five years ago and what you were going through. It's actually quite an amazing thing. The things that worried me eight years ago seem so insignificant now.

List your desires in this moment, great or small.
Example: "I want a hot fudge sundae right now. . . ."

"I need to rearrange the laundry room for better efficiency."

-
-
-
-

Now list some of those things that you could delegate to others.

Example: "My sister can pick me up a fudge sundae when she visits later."

"My partner can help me tackle that laundry room by adding some shelves."

-
-
-
-

Everyone Wins in Their Own Show

My four-year-old, Finn, said this to me one day, "Mom, everyone wins in their own show." He was referring to the fact that we were having our own art show or exhibition and his brother was wondering if we were going to win. I told them we have already won because we worked hard to have the opportunity to have our own show. I mean, have you met any three- or four-year-old kids who have had solo exhibitions in several galleries? I think not. So, "everyone wins in their own show."

We have done pretty well for ourselves, if I do say so! This got me thinking though, that what Finn said has deeper meaning, more substance. The only person you should be competing against is yourself, striving to move beyond your past accomplishments. It gives us a sense of purpose, a reason to wake up to the sun and greet it with a big "good morning," throw off the sheets, and be ready for another round. Celebrate your wins and mourn your losses, but always move forward, learn, and grow.

On the note of competition, I really mean the ONLY person you should be trying to outdo is you. Why? Well, say you and another co-worker were both up for a big promotion for the same position and there was a big presentation that settled who got the job. All you could think about was what they were doing for their presentation, how much time they were spending on it, what innovative programs they were using, who they were sucking up to, what they were talking about in the hall there, and so on. You may be so busy focusing on your co-worker and what they were up to, you even lost sleep about it. The big day comes. You finished your presentation, and you thought you could have done better, but you were too exhausted, and it went just okay. How much time went into worrying about your co-worker? Could you not have utilized your energy in a more productive manner? Could you have used your energy for you? Where your focus goes your energy flows.

Remember, focus on you being you—what can you bring to the table that no one else can!? Focus on killing it because you are awesome and know your stuff! All that time, all that energy, for you, your dreams, your goals. Focus on *you.*

When you start shifting your perspective on how friggin' rad you are and getting to another level of cool, that's when you'll really sing! Above all else, it will save a lot of time, energy, tears, and a whole lotta sleep. You know what?! The real moral of the story is this: we are stronger when we work together, and there are some things you are meant to do and some things you are not. There is enough room for success for all—the sooner you accept that fact, the sooner you will be able to settle into the very best version of yourself. You will find the people and the opportunities that are meant for you. When something doesn't work out, it only means that you made space for that more awesome opportunity to come along and the people who you were meant to work with! Only you can win in your own show!

Eff Up HARD

I know I said this before, but growing up I always felt like I was the joke, or not smart enough, and I did things in my past that we still make fun of today. I've learned to accept that part of myself; I've learned to laugh and just let it go. We are all so far from perfect. What is "perfect" anyway?

The point is, if you are afraid to put yourself out there in the first place you will just never know. This life is terrifying, absolutely horrific, because every moment could be your very last. You needn't worry about all the other stuff, because it should just fall away on death's doorstep.

Just do the dang things and eff up hard, over and over again. Effing up will grant you the privilege of trying something and knowing if you like it enough to keep going. So eff up so hard, with no fear. Afraid of starting a website for that start-up? Afraid of public speaking? Afraid of trying surfing? Afraid of joining the poetry improv for women group? Whatever it may be, you need to start somewhere and that, my friend, will come with a boatload of eff-ups, accompanied by wins.

In 2019 I started appearing more and more in live shows and on video as a way of promoting my new artwork collections. Like I said before, I effed up so much that I literally have hours of content of myself saying half sentences, emitting odd noises, and making strange gestures. I didn't come by making videos naturally, by any means. I effed up so hard that I had a series titled "Friday Night Eff Ups" for my reels. Needless to say, it was the most popular thing I've done on social media. I laughed at myself, because it was funny and I'm not at all embarrassed. I mean, I was a little at first. I have less content for that feature because after a couple of years of doing it so often I've become numb to all the things that made me nervous and eff up so hard in the first place. I can string a sentence together now, high FIVE for that!! Now I have a full-time podcast and have appeared in so many videos I've lost count, and really all that other stuff just fell to the wayside. It's fun and I love that it allows me to connect and collaborate with others. So eff up and eff up hard; I promise it will be fun in the long run and will lead to a world of new experiences.

Things Not Going Your Way Has a Sneaky Way of Benefiting You

When someone tells you that you've done something wrong or not good enough, it is easy to get defensive and just be hot-headed and pissed off! How dare they? I hear that, and we've all experienced this, I am sure, and reacted in ways we aren't exactly proud of. But I want you to think back to a moment where maybe, dare I say it, the other person was right?

Going deep into my archives, I want to take you back to when I was in 9th grade English class. We had a brand-new teacher, Ms. Hughes.

She was young and amazing and a hard-ass! Halfway through the first semester she failed me—42 percent. I'm pretty sure this isn't allowed anymore, but it should be, and I will tell you why. I was so taken aback, surprised, and ashamed. But being pretty type A—but also a pretty lousy student—I took things in a stride; I was going to try my best to resolve my grade.

Ms. Hughes didn't fail me to be mean; she failed me because I wasn't doing my best. I had somehow coasted up to this point. She was passionate about teaching, her students, and Shakespeare. She made me fall in love with *A Midsummer Night's Dream* and poetry. She also got roped into coaching the young women's basketball team, she talked about wearing the right bra, and was interested in our personalities, and becoming strong young women with a voice! She cared, a lot more than I was used to, and she was our friend. She treated us equally and used positivity and passion to lead the way in her class, and on and off the court. I connected to a part of myself I never knew existed, that I was capable of expressing myself out loud through the written word. She made me feel smart, which never happened again from a professor until the last semester of my final year of university.

These educators and individuals who care with all of their being are integral for our youth to form those connections; they have the ability to make this world a better place—they need to be valued more, in my opinion! If Ms. Hughes hadn't cared enough to fail me and help pick up the pieces, I truly believe I wouldn't be writing this to you today and wouldn't be the same creative person who strives to express themselves with their full being.

Instead of throwing your fist in the air and blowing smoke out of your ears, take rejection, take failure, take constructive criticism, and transform it. Take the rejection and say: that wasn't the path for me. Take failure and say: this has prepared me for what's to come. Take a constructive remark and say: this will make whatever I am doing even better because I looked at something from another perspective. Every one of these situations is an opportunity to learn, and to be open to learning and growing. It is one of the most beautiful privileges we have on this earth.

You'll Know When It Is Time to Make a Change

After fifteen years in the art world and many challenging years of finding that perfect gallery, the perfect collector, creating work, busting my ass, and hitting my head against the wall . . . it is a tough gig making a creation, photographing it, posting it online, advertising, writing about said creation, finding that perfect person for your painting who has the money and space . . . the odds are not exactly in our favour here, if you can pick up what Imma puttin' down?! Like I said before, the year I created over 130 original pieces of artwork, most of which were custom artworks (portraits I painted that others requested), I was exhausted and extremely burnt out creatively and physically, and at the end of it all there was honestly not a lot to show for it. My best year ever monetarily, but with the amount of time and effort, emotions, and tears that went into these artworks, it was just not worth it. Not sustainable in any way!

After years and years of this, I knew it was time for a change. I was busting my lady parts trying to keep up and trying to make it work. But I knew I could not do it for much longer—it was sucking every ounce of joy out of my creative gift. I am as stubborn as a mule about to be branded, and it was hard to give up my main source of income. But in order to grow, I needed to take a big ol' leap of faith. Not only was it hard, but also scary. In the beginning, I thought it would be cool if I got paid to draw all day, but I had to admit I was wrong, and the only way that I could have come to that conclusion was to experience it. It was a building block to my foundation of something more.

I decided to sit down and reflect and decide what might work. I had this spark of energy and burning desire to write a book. As I mentioned before, partway into writing, I realized I had been putting this book together for years, through blogging, social media posting, and journaling. It was just me finally deciding to call myself a writer and feeling like I was good enough and worthy. It took time for me to get to this place.

I decided to try a bunch of shit, why not?! One of those things was starting a podcast because I had something to say—many things to say, for that matter. The podcast was a great way to socialize with other creatives from around the globe. Some plans have worked, some not so much, and I've flushed them along with a bit of $$. But my friend Cee, who is a badass in marketing and is now CEO of her own company popped on my podcast one day and said something along these lines: "All businesses lose millions a day; no one sees it—well, some do, it just depends what level you are on. It's harder as a small business because you see every penny that comes in and every penny that flows out." *This* is so true; it's so much more of a challenge because we have the emotion tied to it and all the "try hard" that it took. The losses hurt that much more.

Those losses are lessons, that you either need to adjust or let something go. You just need to hold on to the hope that each path will lead to another, maybe not in the way you predicted or hoped, but you know it's in the right direction and that you need to keep going. Let it all play out, develop patience, and believe that, in time, opportunities will come your way—only when you are ready for them.

When you let go of some of it, that leaves space for what was meant to be there. Don't be afraid to let a few things go. It will feel so damn good. Because all that really matters is that you have the people you love in your life—the other stuff can just fall in line around it. Isn't that what all the great morals of the stories are in movies and books? All that matters is love. Love for yourself, love for your family, love for your life.

Be Your Own Boss

Another great example of a creative I interviewed is child painting prodigy Dimitra Milan. I had her on my *Colour Me Happy* podcast recently. She is extremely successful, selling over $1,000,000 worth of art and products by the time she was fifteen and, being represented by twelve galleries, she had very little control over her business life. She is twenty-two now and she explained to me that she felt like she had lost control, and needed to do this her own way and travel down her own path. Success isn't always what it is cracked up to be. Not when there is a lack of balance. She made the bold choice to cut off an insane amount of income. And, to make a long story short, it worked! She is shining!

She took the reins and has become her own boss and has taken what she knows and shares through herself and her family's institute, the Milan Institute.

Don't be afraid to be your own boss! It can be a lot, but I believe it can be totally worth it!

Find Your Mantra, Find Your Fire

One of the most powerful exercises I've learned in two years of mindset and manifestation work is to create a mantra. To be honest, it has been only a month now that I've had my own—I had some walls in the way. But it took me a long time to come into myself, and all the steps it took to get to creating a mantra were necessary.

This actually all started on an adventure to get some softer sheets. I decided to treat myself to nice new sheets, ones with a high thread count, like in a hotel. This comes back to self-care for me—nice sheets, nice sleep—a treat for me after recovering from a sickness, when I was so soaked with night fevers, I wrecked mine. I picked some up one day and washed and dried them, only to find that they felt like crunchy dried paper towels. Fuck me, no wonder they were on sale! Gah. Annoyed, I packed them back up with the receipt, putting them by the door ready to go back in the morning to spend that extra $30 on sheets that would actually feel like hotel sheets. I thought, *I will go when I am on that side of town next; it's -30 and late, no need to go out now. . . . It's one of those nights where you should snuggle in and work in the studio.* But I got my baby to bed and my partner was hanging out with the other two boys, and I felt this need to go. Something was tugging at me. So I started up my minivan and took off into the dark, snow-covered streets to the HomeSense decor store.

When I drive now, I always sneak in an audio book. Self-help is my favourite: a daily dose is what I need to keep myself motivated. This one was again by my hero, Jen Sincero, *Badass Habits.* The chapter was about how she found her mantra. I arrive at the store fifteen minutes later; I pause Jen. Hop out into the dark parking lot and run through the mid-winter night blizzard, the ice flakes biting my cheeks as I sprint in through the sliding glass doors of the entryway. I step inside the fluorescent-lit store and proceed to return my crunchy, scratchy sheets in hopes of finding cloud comfort like I initially envisioned. Ah, found them. I go to pay and pause at all the trinkets before the till. (I don't have my kids; I might as well take an extra second in the store, in the hopes that my husband has completed bedtime by the time I arrive back home.) While I am standing there in a blind gaze looking at all the mugs with the saying on them "oh for fox sake," this woman comes by with one of those giant-ass push brooms. It was 8 p.m. after all, and they would be closing soon. I move back the 4 feet required to let her pass between me and the mugs. She pauses and looks at me (at this point and time I am all masked up, toque and winter coat and all), and she says to me, "Oh, hey, Brandi, I love your big mural downtown. Every time I drive by it makes my day." WTF. How did this woman even recognize me? I think we went to high school together, maybe. I don't know, because she, too, has a mask on.

I proceed to say thank you so much and that I am working hard to do more around our community, and around the world! I think to myself, *Wow, I didn't know that one mural could be so impactful that I am now getting stopped about them. How beautiful was that?!*

I sprint back through the parking lot, shielding my face from the blowing snow and back into my warm van. All filled with good feels. I pop my earbuds in and turn Jen back on and she proceeds to talk about how she found her mantra and that to find your own, you must play with words, move them around, say them in different ways—not just any words, words that hold deep meaning for you, words that make you feel things every time. I start to think about how powerful my creativity is, and that it can actually impact on a larger scale and improve others' lives so much that they stop and kindly tell me how much it does. What a revelation this was! I start to say it out loud: "My creativity is worthy and powerful!"

There you have it. I found my mantra on the way to randomly return sheets on a cold winter drive in my minivan. I felt that tingle, that pull, and I followed it. Even though it was a pull to drive out at night, out of my routine. A domino effect of small events all falling one after the other, leading me to my mantra. Not a big deal, you say? Yes, big deal!

I say my mantra throughout the day. As soon as I started this practice, opportunities and weird coincidences began happening to me. In just one month my world changed, or maybe my outlook, or maybe both, I don't know, but Imma just gonna go with it! What changed? Faith. Exercising my faith. Faith that where I am is where I am meant to be.

Exercising trust. Trust that any event, big or small, is an essential event, necessary on my path and to my mantra.

My creativity is worthy and powerful!

I close my eyes and imagine that my creativity and joy blasts out of my open arms through my fingertips and flows to the world around me. You know that beautiful rainbow crystal bridge from *Thor*? That's what my joy looks like. Sometimes I envision it as me flying up with wings, twirling and blasting joy and creativity outward.

I genuinely believe that I will change the world with my creativity, and that it all started with returning some motha effin' sheets. It started with me honouring the signs and trusting the tug of the universe.

Once you find your mantra, say it: when you wake up, when you meditate, when something triggers you, when you go to bed at night. Sing it, shout it off rooftops.

Find your mantra!

Close your eyes, play with some words that lift you up—when you say them, they bring you sparkle power and fire. Once you find your mantra, envision that power inside of you. What does it look like? What does it feel like? Does it have a smell or colour? Whatever you discover about your mantra, I know it will impact your life just as mine has for me.

Now write it as many times as needed to let it settle in!

Gratitude for the Green Stuff!

Gratitude is the most powerful thing you can keep in your back pocket. If you are into the self-help world at all, you will already know: everything always leads back to gratitude.

It feels like yesterday, but I guess it's almost been a decade now since I arrived home from university. I came back to my sweet hometown of Lloydminster, Alberta-slash-Saskatchewan (border city—if you were wondering, yes you can stand on the border and be in two places at once). I realized after leaving and coming back that it was important to me to be close to the people I loved. Life was just not the same for me without them near. It is true what they say, distance makes the heart grow fonder. Thank goodness for that. In hindsight, one of the best decisions I have ever made was to come home. Because my partner and I will always have that extra time spent with our parents a few years before we lost them. That time, and those memories, will be treasured in our hearts forever. This is the thing I am most grateful for: time with the ones I love.

Gratitude is of the utmost importance. However, there is something else that we need. Wait for it . . . money. Surprised? So was I! I had some work to do around my money mindset, and here is why:

One: I didn't grow up with a lot of money. We weren't poor, we had a roof over our heads and food in our bellies, and that was enough, but I know my mom only made $23,000 a year and was a single mom with three kids. I actually have no idea how she made that work—she was something special.

Two: I didn't grow up with the belief that I could have a lot of money, run a business, have the lovely things that went along with having a few dollars, because there was just no one as an example of that in my life, and we didn't have a computer in my home until my late teens. No internet equals not a lot of exposure.

Three: The thought of running a business, or being the head of anything, never even crossed my mind.

Four: Society, peers, teachers, and family reinforced that as a young woman you were limited; expectations were set and limited toward basic careers.

To get my point across, there is my partner and husband, whose dad opened his own home building store, Windsor Plywood. My husband, without a doubt, never questioned whether he could own and run a thriving, successful business. It was just assumed that as a young man he would one day either start his own business or take over the family one.

I was the first person on my father's side of the family to get a degree. Wait, scratch that—my dad went to meat-cutting college for a year. The first person to have a university degree, there we go!

It has taken me a long, long time and a lot of work to overcome my money and business mindset. To figure out what it is I really want and what it is I really deserve. I know I had a few jobs where my male counterparts made 30 percent more than I did, and I did twice the job—this still pisses me off to this day. I also know that I will never let THAT happen again.

I realize that I have already surpassed any expectations I had for myself as a young woman. My home now is beautiful. If had seen it as a young woman, my jaw would have hit the floor. With that realization, I began taking my life in through my teenage eyes and seeing how pretty fucking amazing it is and how great I already was at making the money I needed to get here. I already had these skills—gratitude and perspective made me see just how capable I was and am.

And ya know what? After this crazy fucking year of pandemic mayhem, I have had three job offers, and not one questioned my fee or my ability to perform in the position. I worked and dedicated so much time to my brand and my messages and the services I offered, I finally felt confident in my abilities. I have been doing this for fifteen friggin' years and I am proud of who I am and what I have to offer, and I will not be taking any less. I now know that when I say no, it opens up space for an opportunity that was meant for me.

If you are dedicated, if you are driven, and if you know what you want, do everything in your power to make it happen, because the only person who can do this is you. You are good enough. We have all been put here for far too short a time—take advantage of this stunning moment you have the very privilege of being in RIGHT NOW.

It doesn't matter where you are from, how much money you have, who your shitty partner or friend is, whatever—it really doesn't. You are enough. You are here. You have the power to decide. Decide who you are, where you want to be, and how you're going to get there. Because you are enough—I am going to say it again so you get it—I am enough; YOU ARE ENOUGH.

Money isn't some evil character. You won't turn into Cruella if you have it. It is a lovely thing to be grateful for the things we have in our lives. But how can we do more good things, create the life we envision for ourselves and our loved ones? Money. Yup! It's all around us—it's the water we drink, the clothes we wear, the phone we use, the bed we sleep in and the food we eat. And it's okay to want more of it. Make money your pal, and you both can pal around making the world a better place!

This took a lot for me to wrap my head around, and I know that you, too, can accept that money exists and that it exists for you all around. Through the practice of gratitude and knowing you are open to receiving it and knowing what you would like to receive it for. Why am I mentioning this in a book about outlook? Money doesn't buy happiness, but it is essential to have some of it to live the most beautiful life possible for you.

Carefully take in the environment around you and notice that money is all around, and if it is already all around, we are capable of having it—and more of it. Close your eyes and set a small goal that requires a bit of money. Say exactly the amount you need and what you need it for. Feel it. Visualize using the money for that specific purpose. Think about this, see it, feel it, say it, every day until it happens.

Choose When to Work for Free

Unless you are volunteering to change the lives of children or something heroic, choose when you work for free. Although you can actually be paid to do those things as well. The thing I am trying to say here is when you undervalue your services, talents, and gifts, you undervalue yourself. And if you undervalue yourself, people will also undervalue you and you find yourself in a constant wash cycle of selling yourself short.

You are of value; you have value to offer. Give things away out of the kindness of your heart when necessary, but don't devalue yourself. When you do, others will devalue what you are offering. A great way to avoid this in whatever you are offering is to look to others in your field, see what they are charging, and gauge where you should be with the price point of your services.

There is a BIG difference between generosity, collaboration, and gifts. BIG. A gift can be considerate and heartfelt and can be as simple as a thoughtful note. The difference that this makes I cannot describe to you in words. Showing people you care and giving them your gratitude with a thank-you and some love is one of the most important things one can do in this life and those don't cost a thing. Love don't cost a thing, baby!

Steaming Pile of dog shit

Steaming Pile of Dog Shit

Asshats

Asshats. Yes, for the love of all things, you are going to come across a boatload of asshats! What we are going to go over is how you interpret their asshatted fuckery. (I am swearing because asshats have a tendency to trigger a tiny bit of rage within me—I am sure for you as well—and they will always bother us all to the ends of the earth.) Now, let's channel the rage the asshats cause and turn it into something useful. In most cases, I have reacted politely and appropriately to said "asshats" along the way. At the end of the day, if you are standing up for yourself and standing up for kindness, equality, and basic human rights, stand your ground to the end of the earth against all the ASSHATS! I don't think I said asshat enough . . . once more, asshat.

Having a platform, I occasionally have to deal with some troll-like behaviour, and unfortunately racism, sexism, and a few other things. . . . In that case, I report it and move on—no sense lingering. This is not about me; it is about them. I did have one particular email that was extremely mean. I believe it to be linked to an event where I created a custom order for a big company; someone else had placed the order and one of the other employees in the company took a great dislike to the work (which, as artwork goes, just like music, everyone has different taste). This person proceeded to tell me that *the only artwork that was good was highly realistic and here at our type of company we like realism.* I politely disagreed in a professional manner and stood up for artists everywhere (and felt so fucking good about it), of course. Long story short, I received an "anonymous" email a day later—hmmm, I wonder who it was from?! Very unkind words: you suck as an artist, you are an idiot, you are selling bullshit, etc. I won't pour any more of my time and energy into it. And hey, trolls, you know the internet? We can find you on Facebook, fuckwads! Thanks for the email, Brad. You are now the bad guy in my book.

I am confident and seasoned enough in my professional practice and life that I am not jilted by this person's cruel words (well, I mean, I am a human—it didn't feel great). The problem I had was this: there was a possibility that this bully most likely has done this to others (maybe some who are not so sure of themselves). This is where I drew the line. I took action! I used my platform to accelerate my message to spread compassion. Months later I teamed up with a local brand on their launch for a Kindness Wins campaign to raise funding for anti-bullying programming in our local schools. I used this person's negative energy and turned it into fuel to spread joy in my community and in the world! I actually chose to write this book in spite of said asshat, just so I could really prove them wrong and spread goodness all over! LESS ASSHATS PLEASE, more kindness.

It's funny, that same day as that unfortunate phone call with the dissatisfied man, I also had a studio visit from someone who was actually a business owner in that same industry. They ended up ordering three large custom artworks. They repeatedly told me how much they loved my colour use and fun style and to please do so in their pieces! There are beautiful humans out there, remember that! Always keep in mind to be one of those beautiful, kind humans yourself. Thanks for the painting orders, Eugene; you are now the good guy in my book. You don't know how much your support and encouragement helped me that day. Not only that day, but now—you are a compassionate, kind human who lifts others up.

There will always be people who don't share your point of view or have the same taste. We are all unique, and that's what makes life interesting. I guarantee you will have negative encounters and your share of letdowns; I want you to see those encounters and disbelievers. I want you to take that energy, channel it, let it flow like hot molten lava on its way, flowing over those emotions and go and prove them wrong with all the might you possess.

Was there ever a situation in which you or someone else could have chosen kindness?

I want you to also think about what kind of person you want to be in the world. Do you want to be a Brad or do you want to be a Eugene?

Reflect on how you can grow from your experience. Let it fuel your fire!

I Was PISSED!

> *"When you stand up for yourself, you give everyone the opportunity to grow taller."*
>
> – my favourite lady, Jen Sincero

While we are on the topic of asshats—earmuffs for the kids, folks!—I was recently recommended to talk to a female entrepreneur who represents artists and presents them to galleries. I was excited. I was hoping I had found a woman who would believe in me and could lift me up. It has been a beautiful few years where I am finally finding women in a male-dominated industry. Huzzah! But with this woman and this particular case, well, what can I say? It was a complete and utter letdown. I met with this industry professional. She didn't take the time to get to know anything about my art practice or brand prior to our meeting (which should have been a red flag right there). Just to jump straight into it, here are some main points I took away from our two-hour conversation:

- *From what I can see, your stuff is cute.* (Pardon fucking me.)
- *So I see here on your website that you are starting the conversation saying you are a mother?* (Yes, because I am—is there something wrong with that?)
- *It's not like you are going to show in the MoMa or anything. Any gallery is going to look at you and all you're doing with your brand and say no.* (Oh, so I can just be a painter, that's it? WTF. News for you: I already have and have had gallery representation by several reputable galleries; they all love me, and I love them. Go fuck yourself.)
- *Your work can't be purchased by serious collectors.* (I have sold thousands of artworks to collectors globally.)

- *Your collectors will be other stay-at-home moms.* (That's not accurate or acceptable to say.)
- *Maybe you can sell diapers from your Instagram.* (Why?)
- *I think you should take the word "artist" off your website.* (Confused face)
- *Maybe you could get a wine sponsor.* (Oh, okay, so I can promote day drinking. Cool. I am eleven years sober . . . ya, let's get some moms drunk at home with their babies. Seems acceptable, like they aren't going through enough already.)
- *If you are going to pursue an art career, it will be an uphill battle.* (It's already been fifteen years, ya, I know. What job doesn't come with its challenges day in and day out? Fucking bring it on. I've done harder shit than this!)
- *You need to decide what you want to be: a brand or an artist.* (Thanks for the advice; I can be both—that is allowed.)
- *I mean, you live in the Canadian prairies.* (And? I live in the most supportive, amazing community with others who believe in me and support my journey. YES I DO LIVE IN THE CANADIAN PRAIRIES. I guess you live in a better part of Canada than I do? I just witnessed my small city raise $500,000 in twelve hours for a very worthy cause. We are special and proud of where we live.)

At this point, most of you know I am a mother and an artist and so many other things. I know it is unclear to some, but this is what I am, and I am not afraid to follow my path. I am proud to be multifaceted. Not many may have done this, and no one will do this in the same way. But I can tell you *clearly* that I am an artist. I do know there are giant groups of mothers paving their way through the art world. I've met them.

We are friends, and they are stunning and empower one another. It is a very beautiful thing.

The art world is severely underrepresented by females on all fronts (on top of the fact that only 16 percent of business owners in Canada are female—this isn't happening in just the art world). Showing myself creating with my kids in my studio is a great statement. No, we are not crafting—well, sometimes we do, but to be honest I am complete garbage at crafts. Take this morning: our gingerbread house was an epic failure. But it was fun; that is a part of my life, and it's okay that I share that side of myself.

But no, I produce bodies of artwork created by myself with my children by my side, because my artwork is an outcome of my environment. I am and always will be an artist. Our *Gus Series Collection* travelled across the country as an exhibition and installation. We filled those venues with hundreds of people. Why? Because these artworks are filled with passion, love, and narrative and so much more. Artwork is fluid and cannot be defined. If Duchamp can sign and plop a urinal upside down and have it be the most controversial piece of artwork in the twentieth century, I can certainly collaborate with my three-year-old son. My son, by the way, painted our toilet and every other surface of our home. If he is not an artist through and through, I don't know who is. So fuck you, this is art if we call it art.

The worst part and the problem I had with this whole encounter was that it was a woman putting down another woman. Telling her that she wasn't good enough. Have we not yet moved past this? Collaboration above competition.

When we lift one another up, we are stronger and make positive change for those who come after. I certainly abide by those morals.

I want to share with you a poem of mine that accompanied a body of figurative artwork titled *Self Love Collection*:

Mine

One of the first concepts we grasp in life
mine

yet somehow what is mine

as a girl

and now as a woman
had and
has been

Judged

Moulded

lusted after

shaved

plucked

pushed

shamed

mine – stolen
conglomerated
a society obsessed

let them be shamed forever into silence

A door swings open
light crawls across the floor
she walks through

Resilient

unscathed of the injustices
that weighted on her foremothers

– brandi

You know what?! I am a more well-rounded artist, woman, and all-around person since becoming a parent. IN FACT, I feel as if nothing existed to me before this point. My days are filled with more wonder and more joy than I could have ever imagined. I have had the privilege of reliving my childhood through my children's eyes. I got to appreciate my mother and grandmother and connect to their beautiful journey through this life. My friend Tami always says, "Imagine your dinner table. . . . What does it look like twenty years from now? What kinds of things do you want to see? Who do you want there?" I want to see mine filled with my family and my children and their children and laughter and love. Because those are the moments that truly define our existence. But that does not mean I can't have both. What is this, 1952? Have we not broken down this barrier of sexism and rules?

I want to make art about my life; it holds meaning and value.

I already know what the show is called: "Motherhood through the ages." AND YOU KNOW WHAT, MAYBE IT WILL SHOW AT THE MoMA. Maybe it won't, but that doesn't make it worthy or not. AND I can be a mother and paint and write books and paint 135-foot wall murals and teach and do whatever the fuck I want. And that makes one BADASS example for my kids and other young women around the world.

I am stronger because of my kids. Want to know why? Because motherhood has been the greatest challenge of all. If I can push three mini fucking watermelons out of my vagina, I can pretty much do anything I set my mind to. Art world, I am here and I am never leaving. I will find my people who believe in me, who will support me, and I them, and if there isn't room for us now, we will make the room.

So, nice to meet you, lady—asshat. I hope I never speak with you again. Thanks for lighting a grand fucking bonfire under my ass! Oh, and go fuck yourself.

What I did come to realize from this encounter was this: She was not a trigger for me; I somehow was a trigger for her. Something about the way I lived my life didn't sit right with her. That is okay.

I know I am not the only one who has gone through something like this. I want to hear your story; I want to talk about your story. Please reach out—let's get the conversation going. Let's make change together.

Channelling Anger

If you haven't noticed yet, it is pretty easy for me to get fired up. My passion boils right below my skin. I am sensitive and emotional. Those are not flaws, but they can take hold of me if I'm not careful. What I have learned to do is take that energy, which is mostly likely anger, and let it flow.

I want you to be able to turn anger into motivation the way I have. Make it your mission to prove those asshats wrong! Even my own husband was shocked when I declared I was going to write this book, but that didn't stop me. I felt a creative urge and needed to get this all out into the world. I have a voice and something to say and share and spread, inspiring the world to shine as brightly as possible. Even if I help one person, it is worth all of this. It is important to hang on to your why—it will move you forward in times when you need it the most.

Repeat your mantra here.

On social media, I had the unfortunate privilege of being trolled, and when I reached out to my followers to tell them about the incident my lovely, supportive community, *Colour Me Happy,* was there. One of my kind and beautiful members and friends, Tasha, shared with me the words of Theodore Roosevelt:

> *"It is not the critic who counts; not the man who points out how the strong man stumbles, or where the doer of deeds could have done better. The credit belongs to the man who is actually in the arena, whose face is marred by dust and sweat and blood, who strives valiantly, who errs and comes short again and again, because there is no effort without error and shortcoming, but who does actually strive to do the deeds; who knows great enthusiasms, the great devotions, who spends himself in a worthy cause; who, at the best, knows, in the end, the triumph of high achievement, and who, at the worst, if he fails, at least fails while daring greatly, so that his place shall never be with those cold and timid souls who neither know victory nor defeat."*[7]
>
> – Theodore Roosevelt

The thing is, the whole troll or asshat incident . . . I would never take it back. It led to me actually writing this very book. Even as horrible as those people were, for some reason it made me try even harder. I wanted to prove this person so very wrong. Prove them wrong by spreading more positivity and kindness, so we can have less instances like the one I experienced. Trolls and asshats alike, I thank you, I guess . . . because it

[7] Theodore Roosevelt, "Citizenship in a Republic," transcript of speech delivered at the Sorbonne in Paris, France, April 23, 1910, https://www.presidency.ucsb.edu/documents/address-the-sorbonne-paris-france-citizenship-republic.

really was the hot fire I needed to break out of my shell and shatter it all over the world with little rainbow sprinkles of joy!

Bullies

I was once sent to a bullying conference for one of our office learning courses because we had a workplace bully. It was led by a woman who once worked in the White House and who was severely bullied by one of her co-workers. It was an enlightening few hours, and I am going to share with you the CliffsNotes version: there is nothing you can do when it comes to bullies. That was truthfully the long and short of it that I took away from what we learned that day. Bullying is not about you; it is about them. Don't try to be their friend, don't bake them cookies, don't try to discuss a Netflix show you both like at the watercooler. Don't try. Avoid them if you can and go on with YOUR life—YOUR life, because you are no longer going to allow them to be a part of it.

I know that was probably not what you were expecting, or what you'd like to hear. But it actually worked and works. You cannot control others. You cannot control others' actions or behaviours. I also know that there are unique situations and there are programs and counselling if you have encountered severe bullying. There is no one person who has not suffered at the hand of a bully in their childhood and adulthood. I am just going to come back to this: kindness takes less energy; let's be really conscious of where we are steering ours.

What triggers bullying typically is something about you that bothers them to the point that they loathe you for reasons unknown. I repeat: It is them. Not you. Typically, jealousy plays a large part in this. Follow your own path, be true to you. Feel sorry for the bully, because something so toxic lives within them that they are so unhappy they feel the need to put others down.

Somehow and in some way they got to the point where they feel the urge to physically or emotionally hurt others or themselves. Something most likely not so great. Give them space. Feel bad for them. Regardless of all of that, they still don't have the right to hurt you. Stay clear.

Reflect back or on a current situation where you could avoid conflict with your bully or wish them well from the past and move on.

Try Your Best NOT to Be an Asshole (Sometimes You Are Though)

This is pretty self-explanatory: don't be an asshole. On a daily basis, some people can blow your fucking mind. Breathe, don't blow theirs, and move on. If you can't move on, write it down until it doesn't bother you anymore. Or write a chapter about it in your book and drop their name . . . that might make you feel better—it did for me. That's some long-term revenging right there. I'm only joking; those aren't their real names . . . or are they?

The feelings are what really get you: embarrassment, anger, fear. They are the emotions that cause reactions. Take away the emotion and step out of yourself. Breathe. Ask yourself: Am I going to let this take hold of me? Is it worth it? Can I come out of this situation in a better way?

But really, don't be the asshole. Are there things that make your blood boil? Yes. Someone ate your turkey sandwich in the fridge at work . . . we are all allowed bad days, months, or even a year (*Friends* reference for the millennials). But what if we could control those bad days? Take hold of the way we react and move our reactions into action. Action toward our higher selves, our morals, our goals, and our core values.

You never know someone else's story. You cannot assume everyone knows what is going on for the other person. They could be in a hurry; they are on the way to the hospital, or their dog died this week; they could have a million kids and are in a rush to get them from school to ballet. We can't expect ourselves to be happy all the time, and we can't expect everyone to be on their best behaviour all the time either.

We cannot control others. What we can control is how we react, and how we choose to move forward. On that note, don't be reactive; take the time to process the information first, and always choose kindness.

For example: my family and I were recently at our local park ice skating. There was a lady dancing around the park looking quite silly, while another person filmed her. They seemed young, so my husband and I naturally wrote the behaviour off as "those darn kids will do anything for a TikTok video." Which led to me, that same evening, mentioning the dancing lady on a live from my Instagram platform while I was chatting about what was coming up for the new year for our studio. I may have even said I wished she had fallen . . . not nice! Days later, to my genuine surprise and amazement, I got a message from the dancing lady in the park:

> I'm the crazy lady who you caught dancing in the park, that you spoke about on your Instagram live. I don't do TikTok videos, however, I do enjoy sending birthday wishes to my loved one's during these times. Thought you'd like to see the end product. From one local artist to another, I hope 2021 brings you and your business even more success!

Now I ask you: who was the asshat in this situation? Yes! You are correct—it was me.

This was a perfect example of my making assumptions and jumping to conclusions. The dancing lady taught me a very valuable lesson: there are kind ways to approach a situation and there are unkind ways to approach a situation. Not only was I embarrassed, but I also apologized profusely. Moving forward I vowed to work on being less reactive and to stop acting like a jerk and a person who assumes the worst and judges.

In the end, she was actually the owner of a local dance studio. She wasn't mad, to my utter surprise and amazement. But I felt terrible and gave their studio a ballerina painting.

Lesson: there is always room to grow, to learn, and to be better!

I am proud to announce that out of that whole shit-sandwich situation I gained a friend. She taught me that even if it is not warranted or deserved, you can offer kindness and connection.

As far as I know, when it comes to social media, this was low on the totem pole of how bad it could have been. The biggest thing I can take away from the experience is the importance of lifting people up, as opposed to putting them down, and the power of choosing simply to be kind.

Kindness Takes Less Energy

Remember that kindness takes less energy, and it makes you feel good too! My parents were polar opposites when it came to energy. My mom could hold a grudge for years—it was actually a bit impressive, but not that fun to be around. My dad avoids confrontation at all costs unless you use the wrong tool in the kitchen (it's a chef thing).

To help you grasp my parental dynamic, I will tell you a story about the time my mom let my brother and I stay home alone for a month while she travelled to South Africa with her best friend. Leaving my sixteen-year-old self with my four-years-older lazy brother (sorry, bro) at the house. I obviously took advantage of my Mom-less house and threw as many parties as I could. One Saturday night my dad popped by (who the heck knows where my brother was?) There was a full party in motion, and I had made a massive bowl of salsa for all my guests. My Dad walks in and looks around, like whatever, and proceeds to come into the kitchen where I was pouring out a bowl of taco chips to go with my homemade salsa. He takes a chip, dips it into the salsa, looks at me, and states in annoyance, "Brandi, you ruined this whole salsa; there is way too much onion in here."

What about this massive shaker I'm hosting with a bunch of underage kids? Yup, my parents were very different. The neighbours called the cops, but my dad came and left hours earlier, just worried about the salsa. Got to love him.

When it came to my mother and her grudges, well, all I can say is when she held them, I could see that it ate her up inside. When I resort to that grudge-holding behaviour, similar to the way she did, it affects my mood and physical well-being. Keeping those kinds of thoughts and that kind of energy inside can cause you actual pain and stress. Stress is the leading cause of so many ailments. I truly believe you can avoid this if you take a look at it from another perspective, or take a second to ask yourself:

- *Am I going to remember or care about this tomorrow, or the next day, or in a week or a month? Do I really want to engage with an individual who clearly has some shit going? If I confront them, will it end well and is it worth the effort?*
- *If that wacko cuts me off, do I flip them off or do I give a kind word and a wave? What would make me feel better?*
- *What kind of person do I want to be? What kind of energy would I like to radiate?*

My mom used to call my partner and I "The Bickersons" because we could never just keep anything to ourselves and we always said exactly how we felt or what we thought right in front of everyone. One day my mother-in-law said to my mom, "It is really hard to be around and it bothers me." My mom replied, "Yes, it is hard, but I think it would be a lot worse if it was the other way around."

They were both right; we did it to an inappropriate level, but I can tell you one thing: we never go to bed with something unsettled or being upset with one another. If we have a disagreement, which we often do, we figure it out right then and there and move on. We've had thirteen years of practice and had some pretty big doozies, and it's worked out great so far! My mom was right too; it was a bit ironic that she said that, as the biggest grudging grudgerson I've ever met, but it would be unmanageable to hold all that.

Unless you are standing up for what is right and everyone is safe, in most situations it is just healthier to not engage. You can move on, and not let it take up your precious, important time. This is your life—you are in control of how you feel. Think about it; you could save all this energy for something amazing, something that could change your life! Or it might just help you sleep better at night. Just always store in the back of your mind that kindness really does take less energy.

For example, from when my second son, Finn, could open the top of a Sharpie there was permanent black marker on every surface of our home. I mean, we are talking about over thirty different surfaces in our home. Our back door has a big monster face on it. Our toilet is one-of-a-kind! And our walls are to the point where I have totally given up. I was venting about my predicament to my sister and she just told me that it really doesn't matter, let them be kids and paint your walls again in ten years. I could not help but agree with her. So what did I do but go and order Finn a JUMBO pack of king-size black Sharpies.

What do you know, my Finn is one badass tiny artist! I am not just mom-bragging here—his artwork is bold and free! We made a painting collection during the pandemic of thirty-two paintings, just Finn and I! They are all giant shapes that fit together as one painting. We called it Geometrics, and they are covered in black Sharpie ink.

Here were my choices once he could get the pen cap off: a) scold my child day in and day out about his new colouring habit or b) embrace his creativity, encourage his brave and bold choices, and see him thrive at something he is good at.

Encouraging Finn's creativity has given him an outlet and safe space to create and express himself. He embraces his passion, and isn't afraid to be himself. Although he is only five years old, he has taught me many valuable lessons. He has taught me that we always have a choice. And kindness and compassion always take less energy, and let's face it, compassion makes this world a better place to be a part of.

Soul Suckers

Unfortunately, ultimately there are people out there who will suck out your soul, or who just friggin' suck. These people come in many shapes and forms: they ask too much, they are always hemming and hawing, they never give back, they basically drive the bus to a negative town. And it typically takes way too long and many lessons learned before we decide, if ever, to separate ourselves from the suckers. We can call them your "excess baggage," and, in all honesty, they are a lot to haul around.

It is always a difficult decision to cut people from our lives, but if we are to move forward and live a positive and abundant life, we might have to pull up our pants and toss a few suitcases off the bridge. Are you picking up on what I'm putting down here? You will be relieved and surprised at how much time and energy some people can take out of you, and what happens when you remove the CHEDDAH, the CHEESES! FUCK 'EM! You deserve the best of what life has to offer. The most productive method of doing so is moving forward, leading by example, and seeing who hops onto your positivity train with you. It's hard, but it's life, and this is your one shot—take aim and shoot for the stars!

Make a list of some of your goals in life, focus on them each and every day, and march on!

-
-
-

Grudges

Speaking of energy, let's talk about grudges. Sure, there is a time and place to hold a grudge, when it comes to moral integrity and all. But if your neighbour's dog pooped on your lawn, don't go and pick it up and place it under their windshield wiper or anything. Stare from your living room window and wait. That is not a constructive use of your mind and energy. Actually, that might be the best revenge . . . but don't do it.

I was a rotten teen and a pretty rotten little child, very hot and very cold. Like most teens, there were a lot of hormones and weird shit fueling unfamiliar fires. And like most teens do, I took it out on the ones I loved the most. I drank every type of alcohol I could get my hands on and was selfish, a not-thinking-things-through kind of stinker; however, I was a bit sneaky most of the time (I think anyway).

My mom used to send me off to stay in old Wilkie, SK, with my aunt and uncle or my grandma. Of course, I would always meet a few new friends and go off and be a little shithead. Staying out all hours of the night and doing really reckless things—things I am too ashamed to speak about. Ashamed is a big word, but I really truly am, because I sometimes put my own life at risk, as well as those of others. This journey of alcohol abuse carried on from about ages thirteen to twenty-seven, when I hit rock-bottom at an all-time depressed low. I quit when I started taking medication and doing therapy to help with the depression and never looked back. I am proud to say I am now ten years sober and manage my depression through daily exercise, counselling, and meditation. I keep an eye on warning signs and since being a mother, I have never looked back. I found where I fit. I am happy.

Now, as a mother, I can't even fathom the loss of a child. And how selfish I was to put myself in situations where I would risk the chance of death, to possibly put my family through something so insurmountably tragic. I was such an asshole.

Besides this little self-deprecating spiel, I do have a point. Back to one of my summers in the little prairie town of Wilkie, SK. I was staying with my grandma and not only pissed her off but greatly disappointed her with my behaviour. After that summer I distanced myself from her. In my hot-headed teenage mind I was enraged, mostly for the fact that I knew my brother was as equally rebellious when he stayed the summers there and got in zero trouble, and I was pissed about it. But it's really not what matters—equality of sexes doesn't apply when you are being an asshat. These people loved and cared for my well-being, and I was selfish—end of story. I started a big long grudge on the sweetest lady alive.

Time—we are back to time and how fast it goes. My grandma is now sick, and though we have gotten closer since I started having children seven years ago, I lost fifteen years—that is a LOT of years to hold a fucking grudge!!! I am, of course, as stubborn as a mule, but what a colossal waste of time, energy, and pain. She always encouraged my creativity and loved talking about it with me. She taught me to make buns, spent time teaching me card games, and gave me only love. Hindsight is always 20/20, unfortunately. MORAL of this story is, as you probably can guess: Don't hold grudges; life is simply too short. Either move on or forgive.

I don't care who did what and when or how. Move the fuck on.

Are you holding a grudge? Hash it out here; you may just think about letting it go . . . save your energy for the person you would be proud to be.

Choose Your Battles

We are faced in this life with a never-ending reel of choices. Paths that split in either direction. Let us choose the trail that can lead us toward our ultimate goals. Let's choose not to travel down the perilous path that is filled with treacherous turmoil and icy heartbreak. I truly believe in and am consciously working moment by moment on pouring energy into constructive places. Yes, it takes awareness and deliberate effort to decide how to move through the motions of your day. You have a choice.

For example, in the early morning in our household, the majority of my requests fall on deaf ears to the four males I share my home with. In the morning I can shout out requests until the cows come home—Get dressed, Brush your teeth, Grab me your lunch kit—and no one gives a rat's ass! Recently, I've realized that if I just do my things—make breakfast, go on a run, whatever it is—as long as everyone eventually takes on their tasks in a somewhat timely manner, we are as cool as a cucumber. Gus, who is now seven, has been making us all sunny-side up eggs with toast when he gets up, to all my delight and wonder. They are growing, and I am letting go more. Trusting them, empowering their ability to take on life tasks. I am just a bit of a control monster and need to let that part of me go. Why? Because I am using all my great beautiful, fresh morning energy on something that will most likely happen in its own time anyway. Just possibly five minutes after I deemed it to my liking. Everyone is in charge of their own destiny, as my mom liked to remind us during the last month she was with us.

There is something to be said for routine, and I truly believe that there needs to be structures in place, especially for a young family.

However, that does not mean I need to be the drill instructor and drain all my energy and time into how long it takes someone to run and put their socks on or how unfathomably long it takes my husband to do a morning poo. OH, THE FRUSTRATION!

One of the most valuable books I've ever read for getting children on the go in a fun way was *The Happiest Toddler on the Block* by Harvey Karp (this book is packed with gems that changed my life and outlook as a parent). He talks about "playing the boob." And what that means, in short form, is: Don't yell. No one likes it and no one hears you; be goofy, make it a game; it is 100 percent more effective. "I bet I can get my shoes on faster than you and hop on one foot into the van!" It takes a bit of thinking on your toes, but it works almost every time, and they (and you) eventually catch on! This is not only for kids; some of these tricks also work on my husband (not to his knowledge, shhhh, don't say anything). But overall, being a boob is hilarious, and it works, like, a little too well, but it makes everything more awesome, and your kids will love you more, you will love you more, and everyone wins!

So, choices. Choose who you spend your time with, choose where your energy goes, choose how you spend your time, choose what books to read, and choose what shows you watch. How are these going to change your attitude, inspire you to be a better you? Choices. Let's choose the things that will lift us up toward our ultimate goals (which are different for everyone). For me, I want to spend a life full of love with my family and support them through my passions.

Are you going to flip the bird to the old man who cut you off in the Walmart parking lot? I find it better to give a friendly wave and a smile, and not to make eye contact. It is always nice to know you took the high road, that you did your best to turn a shit situation into a friendly woopsiedoodle. But then move on. Be like: "I'm awesome, if they can't see that, whatever," and carry on toward your ultimate goal of an awesome life. Don't spend time brewing, busting, steaming—do it for you, to move forward and live your best life being the coolest cool you! After all, let's take some advice from one of the most iconic, wise fictional characters of all time, Albus Dumbledore. In *Harry Potter and the Chamber of Secrets,* written by J.K. Rowling, he said to Harry:

> *"It is our choices, Harry, that show what we truly are, far more than our abilities."*

Doodle out your magic here

Confetti

Cupcake

Confetti Cupcake

Just Decide

> *"How will you serve the world? What do they need that your talent can provide? That's all you have to figure out. The effect you have on others is the most valuable currency there is. Don't let anything stand in the way of the light that shines through this form. Risk being seen in all of your glory."*[8]
>
> – Jim Carrey

Just make a decision, then do it. It sounds simple, because it is. The hardest part is to decide—the rest will all slowly but surely fall into place. You will be afraid, but put all fear aside.

When I was accepted into two artist residencies in 2011 months apart, one in Montreal and in Paris, you don't think I was like, *Wow, two faraway places that I've never been before, not only that but go alone . . . but, holy moly, what an opportunity of a lifetime. I'm doing it; I don't care that*

---

[8] Jim Carrey, transcript of commencement speech delivered at the Maharishi University of Management, May 30, 2014, https://www.rev.com/blog/transcripts/jim-carrey-commencement-speech-transcript-2014-at-maharishi-university-of-management.

I've never done anything like this at all before. I am doing this, while pumping my fist into the air?

The day before I flew to Montreal, I was terrified, not knowing what to expect. Montreal was huge, oh my. I stayed with my brother at his new place the night before my flight. He had recently moved away from our small city of Lloydminster to Edmonton, Alberta. He was a musician, and I didn't think he was happy when he lived at home, because there wasn't much of a music scene. He had finally found his people, and the culture he so deeply yearned to be a part of for years. He was happy, I could tell.

This was a version of my brother I had not seen before. He toured me around with vigour and delight. Taking me to all the neat spots he had found in his new city. His new thirst for life was absolutely contagious. I just decided right then, at that very moment, "I am going to be like my brother. If he can do it, so can I."

I distinctly remember the day I stepped onto the streets of Montreal, the sights, the sounds, the smells. It was overwhelming and I was worried I wouldn't be able to find my way back to my apartment. I was ALL ALONE, and I had to navigate this city for thirty days solo. Fortunately, navigation was just available on a cell phone and I hit the streets confidently in stride (sometimes headed in the wrong direction and I would have to backtrack, but eventually always found my way back to the dot). I will always remember the bravery it took to do what I did. But really, the hardest part was deciding I could. I got to know myself and what I was fully capable of; it was enlightening and invigorating.

You are capable of pulling off whatever you set your mind to. If you don't know something, you can learn. If you're afraid at first, know that everything is scary the first time, and maybe the second time, but as it becomes more and more common, you find comfort in the familiar rhythms.

Just decide that you can apply for that new job. Just decide that you want to skydive or to not skydive—you can change your mind like I did. (Skydiving seems less appealing now that I am a parent.) Whatever it is, do it now. I have full faith in you.

When you "just decide" to put it all out there, try new things, and tackle your big dreams, PAY ATTENTION. It is a great opportunity to learn pretty darn quickly what you like and dislike. Along the way, beyond your decision to go for it, you will encounter what things you'd love to scrap, and what maybe wasn't meant for you. There will always be a few things that kind of stink with the stuff you love to do, but you will learn to take the bad stuff because you love doing the good stuff! Ya know?

Like when I go on camera. I don't love it. I hate photos. It's uncomfortable, even more so to take a video of the whole encounter. However, I do love connecting and inspiring other people. It warms my heart to the very core that when I put myself out there, I get to make new friends and make a difference. It's a great back-and-forth energy bounce, and I just can't get enough of it. It is the sacrifice I have made; being embarrassed on camera and being myself has allowed me to open up and venture into new, unchartered waters. I'm not scared anymore; I have become excited about the unexpected places the new venture will lead, and if I make mistakes, that's okay. I am learning and know that I will improve over time. Doing the good and accepting the bad allows me to be open—open for more, open to the idea and exciting fact that I am alive. Bring it on!

The lovely thing is that you get to decide. You're the captain of your own ship, the ship that will lead you to where you were always meant to be. One of the best things about putting it all out there and letting your fanny hang in the wind is you figure out the stuff you like and you get to keep doing it. This process is not an easy one—there are so many growing pains that go along with it. It's an emotional journey, but an essential one on the path to finding out who you want to be.

Don't be afraid to take leaps; it is the hardest part, but you must decide. It will seldom go as you had planned, but it will nevertheless move you forward into magical experiences that will surprise you with awe and wonder. You will never get things right the first time, but there is something to take away from each and every experience. They help you grow, and they are what makes you, you.

Making Space

My sister and I both attended a local yoga spin studio called Oasis, and an oasis it was! It helped us heal through our grief from the loss of our mother and was there in whatever way we needed it to be. My sister was a welder, and she fell in love with yoga and soon after that got her training. A couple of years later the Oasis Yoga & Spin Studio came up for sale. She worked for a year to get her shit together to figure out how she would: number one, keep this space in our community, number two, be a permanent fixture in the business, number three, get a small business loan. She is extremely intelligent and hardworking—needless to say, she figured it out.

Then, of course, the pandemic hit shortly after her first year as a new business owner. The pandemic, a time when so many small businesses closed their doors. She somehow found a way to weather the storm and reopen. This is her tale to tell, so I cannot tell you the ins and outs of it all, but I could see her struggling mentally and physically through all of this. I wish I could have helped her, but there is only so much you can do for others.

She had a staff she couldn't keep employed, because how could she? A mountain of debt without an income stream . . . you cannot keep your salaried staff. As any business owner knows, salaries are one of the highest costs. Long, long story short, tensions were high and my sister no longer felt like she jived with a few people on her team. As time went on, the pandemic stripped away those toxic people in her life. She got to start over. She took the time she was closed to make the studio her own, renovating one small space at a time. I was honoured to be a part of this process because I got to do custom murals all over and it was so fun: '80s-themed neon light spin room, baby!

As difficult as this almost-two-year debacle was for her, I know she would never dream of taking it back. She reopened, and yes, it was slow, but she has grown into herself along the way. She had the opportunity to learn what she didn't want her business to be and what kind of people she wanted to surround herself with. She had the opportunity to realize that the people you spend your everyday life with are essential to your mental well-being. She had the opportunity to create a safe and beautiful space for herself. She had the opportunity to find the people who also want to be on this journey with her, and who appreciate the fact that she shows up every day for them. I am so proud of her.

She made space and it hurt—it was hard, and vacant for a while, and that was necessary and okay. She sure as hell learned what she didn't want and rather preferred that empty space to the alternative of working in an unhealthy environment she didn't feel a part of.

It had a way of working itself out; she made the space, gave it the time. She honoured the journey that brought her to this point. Now she calls me every day ecstatic about her new clientele and her lovely staff, and regales stories of how they lift her up and she them. People walk into her business and are so in awe; that in itself is beautiful. She created her own oasis.

Similarly, in 2020 I decided I didn't want to do some of the work I was doing anymore because it was no longer serving me. I was burnt out and the joy was taken out of painting, specifically custom artwork. When the magic is gone you know you shouldn't be there anymore and something needs to change. I tried so many new things—some worked, some did not. I was flying high; I could tell it was contagious, it was fun, and it was exhilarating, but it just could not last. At some point everything had to level out, and I had to come down. Things slowed and I let go of what wasn't working and am looking forward to the journey on the unexpected opportunities that grew out of these changes.

As I write this it is nearing the end of the year, and I have just now adjusted and settled and appreciated the fact that it is okay. It is okay to say no to money. I am settling into this season. I am sitting comfortably with the idea that I was meant to be writing these words, for myself and for you. It is a stunning journey, and I am grateful to be on it. I finally have time to make space for my thoughts and my family. I have tackled a few things I had piled literally into the corners of my home and figuratively into the corners of my mind. I am ready to come back down to earth and find the ground and take the time to replant a few of my roots that became exposed over this strange year. I have made room for what is to come, and I cannot wait to see what will fill this new space. I know I can say no now; I know I can fill that space with something that will bring me joy.

I feel at ease and at home.

What is one thing you can do this month that can save your energy and build trust in your journey?

What is too heavy in your life? Would it be okay if you left it behind?

I'm Exhausted

> *"The belief that taking time off will cause your entire life to collapse is not only unhealthy, but also arrogant (the world will go on if you stop working, you see). If you don't take time off, your body will eventually put its foot down and make you sick. Bodies do it all the time. Stress is a leading cause of cancer, heart attacks, liver failure, stupid accidents, grouchiness, and suddenly not being able to breathe."*
>
> – Jen Sincero

Aside from the obvious health factors, making time to do the things that inspire you should also be a priority because, um, what's the point of living life without them? Where's the fun in waking up at eighty-five years old and realizing you "couldn't find the time" to enjoy yourself? What were you doing that was more important? This is not a luxury reserved for people who are richer, smarter, or less bogged down than you are. It's a luxury reserved for people who take the time to figure it out and choose to design a more fun-filled life.

I believe you should enjoy what you do, and how you SHOULD feel about what you do because you are doing it for the majority of your life. You should love what you do as much as this: I literally hate to take bathroom breaks because I don't want to take the time to stop what I'm in the middle of. There I am again, doing the pee dance in front of my computer or a painting. I am that crazy enthusiastic about what I do and pursuing passion, and you will know that if you chat with me for more than two friggin' seconds.

Just the other day I actually saw someone in the parking lot I had been meaning to message about a collaboration (he's a developer for these very cool homes and I wanted to stage some artwork in one of his houses). Keep in mind, this guy had never met me! So there I am in a parking lot waving him down like, "Oh, hey, it's me. You don't know me, but I have been meaning to talk with you about our imaginary collab that will be the talk of the town!!" Turns out we couldn't stop talking about our businesses and so many more things, and he too was thinking about a collaboration with me. So there you have it, folks. Chase down strangers in parking lots—just kidding! But don't be afraid; the worst thing someone can say is no, and in my personal experience that only happens if something isn't the right fit for you. Move on to the next idea or spark. And maybe what we do together doesn't quite go to what I imagined in my head, but it will be something new; it's exciting and we are stronger when we work together!

I've decided to quit cold turkey, stop this hamster wheel of trying to do what I *think* might be successful and just keep doing the things I do, in my own way, and that will inevitably attract others. I am exhausted by trying to please others. I've done the thing where I wore myself thin and did things I thought I should do, or what other people asked me to do. I didn't make much money and was not happy—okay, Universe, lesson learned! Here I go . . . and as far as taking breaks here and there, I know myself. If I don't make an effort, I will work every day and never see others (unless I run into you in a parking lot, that is). I have made a conscious effort to reach out and book a few mom dates, so I am accountable by someone else to take a breather, a much-needed one! After those dates I am a better mom, a nicer person to be around, and I like myself more. The BONUS of all of this is that I come back to my studio and work with more vigour and more passion.

I've also decided to focus on the things I like to do, no rush, and the way I want to do them. I don't want to be like anyone else. What works for them works for them, period, or maybe they are miserable. It doesn't really matter. I am setting out to do the things I WANT to do, in my way. If people don't like it, oh well, too bad, take it or leave it, sister! I am pretty sure this will be an easier and more manageable way to live and may just be the true road to happiness.

What makes you really truly happy, like over-the-moon, all-you-can-think-about, why-you-get-out-of-the-bed-in-the morning kind of stuff?

Also make a list of some things you hate and how you can maybe not do them anymore!

Example: LOVE: I love inspiring people through my creativity, being a mom, cooking, and making art.

Example: HATE: Cleaning bathrooms! Made money with my art to pay cleaners to come once every two weeks to clean all house surfaces and bathrooms. Payoff: I get to paint more and clean less, which equals more money, and soon I will get them to come once a week—HAPPY FUCKING DAY!

We Are Far from Perfect, Accept That

Like I said before, we are all human, imperfect by nature. We cannot always say or do the right thing. Believe me, I know. I know over and over again, I know. If you've ever witnessed my failures on social media or in my podcast interviews, you get what I am saying: and now you can go check . . . are you back? There you go, you get it now. I cannot help my blunders, so I just leave them in. I've accepted them in all their forms.

I've actually come to enjoy seeing them—they are genuinely funny. In the past, my mistakes were something I tried to control, and to no avail. They would just happen—I am who I am. I will no longer attempt to hide it or apologize for being human. I'm placing one of those brown, pokey straw-like mats on my doorstep that says "welcome, flaws, I love you."

Accepting my flaws was not always the case. . . . My friend interviewed me for his podcast years ago. I believe I was pregnant with my third child, Teddy, or maybe my second child, Finn—those pregnancies all blur together after a while. Who knows? I was pregnant—there. My friend's name is Shaun and he is amazing and his podcast is special and he passionately and bravely took himself on a new adventure in this life, and I am so proud of how far he has come since that day in my basement studio.

I was one of his early interviews, just when he was getting started. He is extremely established now. I am not surprised; he is one of those people you could sit and chat with for hours on end. After our interview he said, "Brandi, you should definitely start a podcast; I think you'd be great at it." He saw something in me that I couldn't yet see myself. I immediately said, "No way, not for me. I don't like interviews, I hate cameras, and I am good in my little corner of the world painting by myself and not messing up." He then went on to tell me that is all fine and dandy and continued, "Brandi, you can only just be yourself, and that is good enough. I think you are amazing, you can inspire others, you have something to say, and people will connect with that." A year later my videographer friend Kim called me up one day and said, "Brandi, I think we should make a podcast," and you all know the end to that story. This is why it is so important to find the people and the environment in which to thrive. Find all the lids that fit your pot. Because you will all move forward together, cooking up a storm!

The Grass Is Always Greener

In life there is no doubt in my mind that sometimes you draw the short straw. Shit happens. And then shit happens again. Or maybe a few great things happen here and there. Like Mark Manson says in his book *The Subtle Art of Not Giving a F*ck,* "Everything sucks some of the time." He's 100 percent correct for so many reasons. The grass is always greener, la la la . . . but seriously, your day is filled with good and bad, no matter who or where you are. The only thing you can control is your outlook and perspective. No one's got it better than you; it really boils down to what are you happy with, what is that line for you? You are a victim of your own circumstance. You will find some of the happiest people living on the street. Opposingly, the most miserable people with huge offices on Wall Street. The person on the street is tied to nothing and they roam the land seeing the world. The person with the big office, a house, and a holiday home is depressed because they never get outside, work every night until midnight, and don't get to see their family. All outsiders see is the person on the street, weathered, worn, unwashed clothes, and they think that person must be going through a tough time. All outsiders see in the person on Wall Street is them cruising in their fancy car—that person's got it made in the shade with a glass of lemonade! Am I right?! Isn't that what we assume? Green grass.

Our day is filled with demands and challenges. It's about how well we can take the punches and see our lives for the beautiful gifts they are.

Close your eyes and think about three things you are grateful for in your life at this very moment.

1.
2.
3.

More on Green Grass

The best example I can think of from my own life is when I worked at our local theatre doing promotions and hospitality for the acts that came through the stage. I met several big names and a lot of groups on the road. Meeting these groups and individuals was a surprising and interesting experience. I learned a lot about perspective and the basic concept of seeing things through another lens. Many of these people were well-known and "famous." But seeing their lives behind the scenes was a complete eye-opener, to be honest. Most are touring around on a bus or a van stuffed with so many people who have spent too much time together and are, for the most part, miserable. I couldn't imagine being away from home so much and being in a car, a bus, a plane, and then performing all hours of the night just to wake up and do it all over again . . . tough gig, right? I think they get to experience the highest of highs being on stage and the lowest of lows, and for them doing what they love just a little bit is worth all the other stuff. But really, what it says, is maybe you do have it all—you're just not looking at it from the right angle.

One particular famous Canadian rock band came through who was a great example of a tired group of people who had been in close quarters for too long, touring for too many years. In the middle of the very busy day of making sure everyone was running on schedule and happy (which is a bigger, more exhausting job than you may think), my manager decided he didn't need to be around that day (another story for another time). I really think he "decided" not to show up because he had booked an opening act without telling the headlining band, cool cool cool (and the band's manager was out for blood). Reflecting on the events of that day now, walking into it, I had little to no chance of success in making this group happy, although I was ignorant to what had gone on prior to their arrival. In a few hours I learned what all the hostility was about, but it sure didn't make the day any easier or that evening. I got yelled at over a missing bag of candied nuts. NUTS!! What in the great fuck?! Ya, turned out their sound guy ate them . . . weird, someone from your crew ate the food on the table.

Oh, and turning the sound down for the opening act is a real thing, by the way—they sound shittier than the headliner, and I think it is a garbage thing to do. There is enough room for everyone to succeed in this life; lift one another up and everyone wins. But this was a crap day that could have been really cool if that old touring group got over themselves and my manager didn't suck. The opening act was so excited to meet some of their idols and instead learned they were assholes. Not cool, right? Overall, I was let down and learned that fame really isn't everything.

The moral of this story is this: if you aren't enjoying what you are doing for your job (which you do for a big chunk of your life), you will become mean and petty and a lesser version of yourself. I will say this again and again: time is our most precious commodity; stop wasting it being a miserable fucking prick and yelling at the woman who spent the entire day cooking you a homemade meal because she knew how much being on the road sucks and you get fed a sandwich tray and rotten fruit far too often. Basically, I always went above and beyond because I did like my job, and, for the most part, people appreciated the homemade food. And I always picked out all the brown M&M's for the bands—old music reference. Van Halen used to request all the brown M&M's be removed, not because they didn't like them, but to make sure their tech requests and hospitality rider had been thoroughly looked over—they wanted to ensure all the equipment was handled properly, etc., for the show to go on safely with as few technical issues as possible, without a hitch, and no one would die or anything. I believe there is a rumour that at one of their performances the stage collapsed and $80,000 worth of equipment was damaged or something. Anyway, that's why no brown

M&M's was a requirement for their hospitality rider, and many performers are similarly just as demanding. But it's alright. They are entitled to eat good food, be safe when they perform, and have a smooth sailing show. I am sure they deal with a lot of shitheads in their line of business.

I do get it—there are so many working cogs when it comes to anything. Two sides to every story, or many sides, no doubt. But when you come in guns blazin', you're missing out on an opportunity to: A) meet new, cool people; B) have a positive experience; and C) enjoy yourself and just have a good day.

Be kind, always—choose kindness.

In this same job, I got to meet some amazing women I have idolized since childhood. Jann Arden was so funny and so tiny, to my surprise. I towered over her, and she bought one of my portrait paintings I made of her. Over Twitter, ya'll—so crazy! Her manager emailed me a year later telling me how they still talked about the amazing meal I cooked. It warmed my heart. AND Buffy Sainte-Marie, an icon, like, insane, right?! She was a firecracker and had the most energy of any seventy-year-old I had ever met. I also made her a painting and she was over the moon about it, headed straight back to the bus to put it away after I gave it to her! So don't be an asshat if you can help it; it's way cooler and waaay more fun to be kind!

I think about this movie a lot, the one where everyone forgets who the Beatles are after a worldwide blackout. Hold on a sec, I will just Google it here . . . *Yesterday*!! Not sure why I couldn't remember that, ha! You should watch it; it's great, easy . . . maybe watch it before you keep reading, because I'm going to give it away a bit. There is a struggling musician named Jack and he is about to quit music until BOOM—blackout. He gets hit by a bus on his bike, he wakes up in the hospital, and a few days later sings a Beatles song for his friends. They all think he wrote it, and he soon realizes that the Beatles band never existed in this post-blackout world. He starts playing the Beatles songs for everyone and becomes uber-famous after Ed Sheeran hears one. Jack is at the peak of his fame, and the whole time you can tell this isn't really what he wanted after all. He sees that fame is empty, especially when it wasn't honest; it left a hole in him. He realizes that all he really wanted was love and his music, and it had nothing to do with fame or success and that those things were right in front of him the whole time. The movie ends with him playing "Ob-La-Di, Ob-La-Da" back in the classroom, teaching music, where he gets to make an impact on the lives of children every day of the week.

I have lived through the wanting of likes and follows, and after I've been on this road for years, what do they all really mean, what do they amount to? It did help me sell my work, and it allowed me a platform to share my creativity. But it really only does that to a certain extent now. I have chased the idea of money and success. It only actually got me further from it all. It made me an ugly, frustrated and hard-to-be-around person. It was hard to even tolerate myself. It was a nasty hamster wheel I was caught up in. It sucked up my time into a black hole of nothingness, and I never want to go back. I am grateful I have always felt this way, but I haven't always been able to avoid the pull. I love the friends I've made through those platforms. But I am a post-for-work-and-get-off kind of gal. It is frustrating to watch others sit on their phones as life happens around them. Actually, it's not just frustrating—it's sad.

Close your eyes and take a few deep breaths.

What is it in your life that brings you the most joy?

- Going on adventures
- Being in nature
- Olaf.
- Litty
- Watching Olaf play
- Dancing
- Being part of someone's change (helping them heal)

Now imagine waking up in the morning in the perfect place.

Where is that? Cabin on a lake in the mountains

Who are you with? Husband & child.

And what are you going to do with the rest of your time?

Be Brave!

Life is full of trials, tribulations. A balance of joy and lust and hate. But what would life be without those subtle and treacherous balances between good and bad? For one cannot exist without the other. Be afraid, be mad, be hurt—feel all those things, but then charge them with your full force and say, "I accept you; you will make me resilient and strong, but I won't let you stop me. I am going to be BRAVE."

We should just refer to this area of the book as "Brandi's favourite movies." I'm bringing up my all-time favourite film, ALL-TIME, and it's called *About Time*. It has Canadian actor Rachel McAdams in it. If that doesn't make you want to watch it, I don't know what can—she is amazing. The movie is about a young man whose dad lets him in on their family secret, that at age twenty-one all the men can time travel. No, this is not some weird sci-fi movie, not even close. It is about stripping down life to the bare bones. It is endearing and heartfelt and about love and loss. His dad's best advice to him is to travel back to the previous day to live it again, without all the stresses and anxieties that a day can hold, and pause to enjoy a moment or engage with a person or make light of an encounter.

I am a blubbering mess when I watch it, but it hasn't stopped me from rewatching the film twice a year. You will laugh and you will cry and feel all the feels. This is one of my favourite quotes from the main character in the movie, Tim:

> *"And in the end I think I've learned the final lesson from my travels in time; and I've even gone one step further than my father did: The truth is I now don't travel back at all, not even for the day, I just try to live every day as if I've deliberately come back to this one day, to enjoy it, as if it was the full final day of my extraordinary, ordinary life."*[9]

You know the days where birds are chirping, the sun is shining, and there is a soundtrack playing in your head—you can't get enough, ain't nothing gonna break your stride sort of day? We all have these. They are amazing, and such an incredible gift; however, they don't happen very often, and if they did, they wouldn't feel so darn special. I'm going to call these our *be brave days*.

try this! I want you to take your *be brave day* and do everything you've been afraid of or avoiding: message that person you have been meaning to, submit that proposal, tackle your Monica closet (another *Friends* reference). I want you to take that day and slay the hell out of it, because you don't know when your next one is going to pop up. Shout everything you have been holding in from the rooftops! Because goodness knows you won't tomorrow, because you will be so darn pooped from all that you tackled in this one amazing day, the day where you sang "MMMBop" out loud because you were feeling the world behind you!

THIS WILL WORK. Some of it won't, but for the most part, I try to use all the energies of the day I am feeling and rocket launch them into the universe. I'll let you in on a little secret . . . I have a few of these days

[9] *About Time*, directed by Richard Curtis (Universal Pictures, 2013).

every month, and I do so much and ask for so much that I literally forget some of the things I've asked for. It's really great, because then there is less disappointment over putting all your eggs in one basket for that one opportunity. Fast-forward three months and you get an email about this amazing opportunity to work with so-and-so or make a big sale or (insert your good news here). So go for it—be so brave so often that you can't keep track of all your brave moves!

I have never gotten a job I didn't ask for. The first mural I painted was HUGE and on an exterior wall of a downtown business. I began with the decision that I wanted to paint a mural. *Hmmm, who knows people downtown?* Contacted my friend Jill, CEO of Red Bicycle Communications. "Hey, Jill, know anyone looking for their wall painted downtown," and wouldn't you know it, she did. Three months later there I was tackling a giant wall, doing something I'd never done before. It all started with one brave decision, followed with conviction and some hard work. I am permanently a part of my community and helped one business turn its wall into a thriving destination where 10,000 people visited last year alone! Pretty darn cool!

The first step always starts with you. So, capitalize on your positivity and your bravery, and people and opportunities and beautiful moments will be attracted to you like flies on honey. The best way to capitalize on your brave day is to have (wait for it, can you guess?) an ongoing list of the things you want and the opportunities you'd like to come your way. Write them DOWN!

Make a vision board on Canva or a list of all the things you want for your brave self!

- ask therapists for referrals
- disagree with someone
- say no to someone w/out an explanation
- tell a man I like him
- flirt with a man
- start my Youtube channel again.
- ask a friend to go on an adventure vacation with me
- start process for IVF or fostering
- move to mountains.
- not ask for advise
- Look at my finances!
- get my nails done (spend $ on fun things)

Ignite, BOLDLY

There is no later, only missed opportunities—later is now! As I mentioned earlier, when I thought of my title for this book and the first few bits, I was in the middle of a therapeutic massage. I kept repeating the title over and over in my head, afraid that it would float out and pop like a bubble. I was holding dear to my initial intro sentences, and finally I realized I could lose these thoughts into the abyss. I stopped the masseuse mid-massage and asked her to pass me my phone so I could make a very embarrassing voice memo, while naked on the table right in front of her. Was it worth twenty seconds of embarrassment? Yes, it was. For the obvious reason that you are reading this book of mine right now. Don't ever let your magic sparks fizzle away. If you just let those thoughts go, they may never be with you again.

What are some ways to capture your magic? If you are a writer, for instance, you would carry a notebook with you everywhere you go and keep one beside your bed and have a recorder always available for your fleeting thoughts. Let me tell you frankly, I didn't even know I had the desire to write a book; it came to me at that moment. My eyes were closed, I was in a meditative state, and the universe spoke to me, and I wasn't about to run away from this calling.

It was actually a very inconvenient time in my life to start writing a book. I have three boys under the age of six, two of them at home with me during the day (and all night, of course). I am a visual artist and have my exhibition schedule planned out for two years. Very, very poor timing! Why, oh why, did the desire pop up to write a book? But since I began, I cannot even bother to turn on the lights in my art studio where my desktop computer sits. I have so many things to say, I cannot get them onto the page fast enough. When I run in the mornings, I have to make multiple voice memos along the way; chapters keep appearing on the page from the crevasses of my mind; this spark, this idea, my words are soaring out of me and I am unable to contain them!

I am embracing what Elizabeth Gilbert describes in her book as "Big Magic" (I highly recommend you read her book, if you haven't already). She speaks of a man she shared a job with at a university, poet and professor Jack Gilbert. She went on a mission to find out more about this fascinating man, and here is what she found:

> *"Who was Jack Gilbert?*
>
> *Students told me he was the most extraordinary man they'd ever encountered. He had seemed not quite of this world, they said. He seemed to live in a state of uninterrupted marvel, and he encouraged them to do the same. He didn't so much teach them how to write poetry, they said, but why: because of delight. Because of stubborn gladness. He told them that they must live their most creative lives as a means of fighting back against the ruthless furnace of this world.*
>
> *Most of all, though, he asked his students to be brave. Without bravery, he instructed, they would never be able to realize the vaulting scope of their own capacities. Without bravery, they would never know the world as richly as it longs to be known. Without bravery, their lives would remain small—far smaller than they probably wanted their lives to be."*[10]

Every darn time, every darn time, I read that, tears leak, build, and pour over from the wells of my eyes and glisten down my cheeks in glorious streams. Living does take bravery, and you have to try super-hard all the time. It is exhausting, though nevertheless exhilarating, and

[10] Elizabeth Gilbert, *Big Magic* (New York: Penguin Random House, 2015), 6.

so very worth it. I try hard, I try so hard, because there is just no other option. Why else would I be here? Why would you be here? What would the point of all this be?! But to charge the ruthless world head-on and shine with all your glory like a phoenix reborn, bursting from its ashes.

Now, just give me a moment to blow my nose and gather my composure.

I'm back.

Let me ask you, what is stopping you? What is stopping you from baring your soul to the world and living life to its full potential? Frida Kahlo was severely injured in a bus accident and held a brush in her mouth to paint her body that was fully casted. Let's live like that. Let's not let anything get in the way of passionately making our way through this beautiful, chaotic world.

Dream BIG

My dad was always a dreamer and a doer. Although his execution wasn't always spot-on, his heart was always in it. I am going to share with you a story from when I was a child. In the tiny house where I grew up, we had huge, beautiful trees and a lush yard. In the front yard there was this massive evergreen tree, like 30 feet tall. BIG! My dad wanted to make it into a giant holiday tree one winter. I watched him for a whole day attempting to string on the coloured glass lights, sometimes tossing them up as high as he could, and to no avail—they would fall down and some would pop and he would replace them. He even did a few runs to the store for more bulbs. Finally, nearing the end of the day he found one of those golf ball retrievers that were 25 feet long (he didn't golf, so I really have no idea why that was in our old red shed). My dad attached the lights to one end and proceeded to pole-vault these lights half-assed up and down, up and down (not around) the tree. In the end, he didn't have enough stringed lights, so the tree was only partially covered. But he wanted to make this a big holiday tree for his kids and, by gosh, he did it! There was nothing that could have stopped him.

My dad is like, oh, sixty-five or something now, and he just stopped working, because the pandemic hit and there were no longer crowds of 200 to 3,000 to feed at his place of employment. My dad being forced into retirement has been such a beautiful gift, because now we get to enjoy him slowing down. This man worked twelve- to sixteen-hour days up until this point and intended to keep going because he was passionate about his line of work.

This work ethic and drive lives within me; I recognize it. I can't stop and I won't. I am miles from where I started, and I know I can achieve whatever I put my mind to. Why? Because I believe I can, and I try every single day, putting a little mustard on everything I do! And yes, some people have told me I can't or that I suck—not often, but it happens, and my work by no means is or will be perfect. The only person I want to outdo is me. If I am moving forward little by little toward a larger picture, high five to me. If I look back at where I was five years ago, I would have been blown away if you told me I'd be here. Heck, even if you told me I'd be here last year, I would not have believed you.

The funny thing I've realized is that dreaming big requires an open mind. You have to decide what you want and organically accept that it might change or mould along the way. You definitely won't guess how your dreams will come into fruition; you just have a solid ongoing faith that they will. All you can do is show up, be open, be excited. Really though . . . just show up. Show up and decorate a 30-foot effing holiday tree as if your life depends on it. It won't be perfect, but at least you can say you tried. And if it doesn't work, dust yourself off and try again.

Close your eyes and visualize one big dream happening to you this year. Insert it into your life. How will you feel? What will it look

like? What will it feel like? Think about how you will react when it happens.

Outlook & Community

Now, back to the beginning. Remember how I told you I couldn't wait to leave the place where I grew up? Well, guess what? I came back. I live right here, in that same place. I have made the choice to be close to my family and to raise a family here. I could list forever why this place doesn't fit the ideal version of what the lifestyle of an artist and creator should look like. But what I have learned, and what I have accepted and embraced, is this: the sunsets here go on for miles, the skies dance, alive and open, and I bask in all its glory. It is a constant reminder that our lives are small but momentous all at once; it is equally as breathtaking as the rolling countryside in France. I found beauty in my home. I grew up, and I learned to appreciate something that was right in front of me the whole time. Because it is my home—nothing else can replace where you feel accepted and safe. Home is wherever you make it.

We have grown a creative community—out of the vast, stretching prairies, we have found one another. We work together as a community, not limited by where we live, but empowered by it. Our community supports each other and takes pride in what we create together. Every new beginning is an opportunity. Every blank wall, every street corner is a place where I can express myself through my creativity and beautify my city. My community has given back friendships and support.

Never make assumptions and never place limitations on yourself or others. Look around. Be grateful. Never discount what you have right in front of you. One day what you have will smack you in the face with the ugly reminder that the only thing that is constant in this world is time, and what you had is gone. Open your eyes and ears to the opportunities knocking at your door right now.

Oh, Canada

I can fondly remember sitting on the couch with my mom in 2013 (her favourite place to hang and make me watch whatever SHE wanted to watch on the TV). We were watching the Juno Awards, and Canadian songstress k.d. lang was inducted into the Canadian Hall of Fame. She gave a speech that I will remember for the rest of my life:

> *"I think the fact that I am standing here receiving this award says more about Canada than it does about me, because, only in Canada could there be such a freak as k.d. lang receiving this award. Only in Canada could there be people like Stompin' Tom Connors and Rita MacNeil! So, I am here to tell you, my friends and my countrymen, that it is OK to be you. It is OK to let your freak flags fly. Embrace the quirkmeister that is inside of all of us. And I'm not even just talking artists, every single person in this nation has the right to be themselves, live life, go team go, I love you, Canada, thank you so much."*[11]

I still bring up this video to watch every few years. I watch it because this is evidence of how someone stayed true to who they were. k.d. lang held on to who she was and followed, fought, and worked to make her visions and passions succeed. She did so without compromise. And in doing so inspired others to do the same. Live your life for you and no one else. Let your freak flag fly in all its glory.

---

[11] k.d. lang, transcript of speech delivered at the Juno Awards of 2013 at the Brandt Centre, Regina, Saskatchewan, April 20, 2013, https://www.huffpost.com/archive/ca/entry/kd-lang-juno-speech-2013_n_3129280.

No One Can Do This but You!

That's it. No, not really. As an artist and creative, I waited for years to go for the things I wanted or desired, thinking I needed a gallery or that magic person to come along to make all my artistic dreams come true. For years—years—I thought it had something to do with someone else. It just doesn't always happen quite like that. You set your intentions, you live out your dreams. You ask for the things you want and you go out and get them yourself!

Want to write a book, write one. Want to be a painter, buy some paint. Want to learn a different language, get an app. Want to win the lottery, buy a ticket. Just do it. No one is going to come knocking at your door and do it for you and give you the golden ticket to the life you've been daydreaming about.

I was being interviewed for the *I Like Your Work* podcast and host Erika b Hess had me live on their Instagram. I will never forget what she said to me. "Brandi, you know what I love about you, is you just do things." I thought, *Hmmm . . . do I? Doesn't everyone?* And I probably didn't always. In fact, I think becoming a parent and losing one all at the same time made me truly find value in every single moment, and not waste any time and go for it! In all honesty, it forces you to REALLY slay your free time, which, if you are a parent, you know a free moment occurs few and far between. AND when you get that time, you really utilize it to its full potential with pure gusto parent power!

Take leaps, do the things that send tingles down your spine and do the things that give you butterflies. If you're not feeling the fear and the magic, then you're not reaching high enough. This life is exciting and, let's face it, we aren't here forever. Cartwheel your ass out of bed and go do it for yourself!

I can't make changes in your life—that is a false promise. Only you can do that. My only hope is that this is inspiring enough to light a little fire under your ass to be the best version of yourself by your own standards.

chocolate

torte. with

raspberries

on

top

How can we work through this:

* foster
* $ in investments.
*

Chocolate Torte with Raspberries on Top

Motherhood: Time Is Our Most Precious Commodity

> *"I knew immediately that I was a mother the first time I saw her. Even if I had to forget everything else."*
>
> – Brandi Carlile

In 2014, I lost my mother. I was six months pregnant at the time. In losing my mother, I lost a part of myself. My sense of home, my sense of security, my advisor through troubled times. This was not something that could be fixed or repaired; the pain just fades a bit over time and there are fewer and fewer instances where you double over with grief, and you smile at a memory and treasure it instead of sobbing.

Now, I want to speak about becoming a mother, amongst the mess of losing mine, all within an alarmingly short amount of time. I can tell you that without the birth of my first child shortly following my mother's death, I don't think I could have made it through that grief unscathed. Gus, my baby, was my focus and Carly, my partner, was my strength. Never do you truly know the will of what it takes to be a parent until you are one. A child takes all of you, maybe even a bit more. You really begin to appreciate how amazing your own parents were or are.

That experience and shock of death awoke something in me. I had a new thirst for life. Nothing scared me anymore. Nothing could be more painful than losing my mother.

When my mother found out she was sick, she knew she had little time left. I know this was the hardest thing thus far in her life that she had to face. It was deeply painful for her. She was a valiant woman who spoke with intention and purpose. And rarely, if ever, did she speak about her cancer. One of the most beautiful gifts (not necessarily in a physical sense) she left me were letters and notes. She saved all her old letters that she exchanged with friends and her sisters in a box. Gifting me the opportunity to know her before she was my mother. She was smart, funny, and full of wit!

She also left me little mementos with notes on precious objects attached with a letter to myself and my siblings. You may ask why I am sharing something so personal with you. It's because my mom had the rare opportunity of time before she passed, and she used it with all of her heart. She had the sad but courageous opportunity to share some of her personal insight, experiences, and life lessons, many of which I bring into my day-to-day life. Her notes were left with purpose, sharing from her experience in this life what values were the most important. I am going to openly share her note about having children.

Congratulations Brandi and Carly
to the new baby "Hofer Classen"!
I'am sure that the joy and pleasure
they bring will far surpass any
other of your life experiences! May
the fish gods be good to all of
you!
Love Grandma Love Mom
XXX OOO XXX OOO

There was such a warmth my mother provided, not just for her children, but for all of the people she let in. She was a very private and humble woman, extremely intelligent, and full of incredible strength. She was also very scary sometimes, but in the best way, because you knew she wouldn't let anyone ever hurt you. She was also a very talented photographer, fascinated in people and portraiture. And I can understand where my interest in portraiture and people as a subject matter in my art stemmed from. Then there is my father. He is a kind and loving man. And I can never recall a time in my life when he told me I could not do something just because I was a girl. Both my parents were supportive and open, and instilled in us that the things best valued in this life are moral integrity, equality, love, and kindness. Trust me when I say that my siblings and I had some crazy ideas and cockamamie schemes, but there were no bounds on our dreams.

Art & Motherhood

As an artist, I was torn. Creating requires time and headspace. Something I struggled with, especially when my second baby boy came along, FINN. After all, I was foremost a mother. I had given myself over to my children. I needed them, they needed me. But there was just a huge part of me that longed to create, and I wanted to somehow pass this gift on to them. There was just no way I could tackle the solo act of painting that I used to carry on before parenthood—we just don't get four-hour stretches of free time, like, ever! AND I finally figured out a way to do that! It just all of a sudden clicked!

One day Gus's interest in painting and playing in the studio grew. We started working together more and more while his brother napped. I brought in things he was interested in—cars, dump trucks, different tools—and we moved them all through the paint, dumping, splashing, spraying, and having the time of our lives! In turn, the GUS Series was born. A forty-four-piece art series of paintings of local parents and a full interactive installation that travelled to three venues across western Canada. Gus was involved in every step of the painting process from beginning to end.

After losing my mother and father-in-law in a matter of a few years, my belief that time is our most precious commodity grew exponentially. Moments are fickle and fleeting. We should spend them with the people we love—our families. I refuse to lock myself away in my art studio alone and not include my children in my passion for the arts. I want to show them the beauty of mark making, dancing, and expressing yourself with a brushstroke or a splash of paint. I want to teach them that it's okay to make a mess. "YES, Gus, you can step in the paint, squish it between your hands and toes." "No, Finn, you can't eat it." I know that the whole process has been so precious because I have never seen so much joy pour out of my sons! They are confident, self-aware, and playful when creating. Every moment I have spent with them has been worth it, and I can always look back on this time in our lives with absolute fondness. We still, to this day, spend time creating together. We have come out with several collaborative collections and bodies of work. The artwork is unique and has an unmatched energy.

This is one of the gifts of being open-minded to the idea that you may think you know how life is going to work but that's not how life actually happens. I may have thought art needed to be one thing, the way people expect it to be, to fit into an art world standard, but it didn't, and it doesn't. Being open to making art with my family allows us to discover and play and connect to a part of ourselves we never knew existed. It has also inspired countless parents to do the same, and that is the greatest gift of all.

"Finally there's my greatest success. I am lucky enough to be a mother. And I'm still continuing the journey, relearning how to

be truly safe in the world. And it isn't what I thought, it's not by avoiding pain in life, that's impossible. It's in knowing that safety is in vulnerability not in armour. It sounds counterintuitive, but it's true. Life takes each of us to the anvil, shapes us with fire and hammer. Some of us break, while some of us become stronger, more able to face the day. Even happy."[12]

– Jewel

It's true, after these losses, there is reflection, and knowledge to be had from the experiences. I have reformed the way I live my life, my every day. Not from avoiding that pain and grief, but from feeling it. Having it as my constant reminder to be here, be here and be a good parent, a good friend, a good partner, and a good person. It has shaped who I have become and who I choose to be.

Go with the Flow

Someone referred to me as "chill" once. This made me laugh, very hard. If this person lived inside my brain, they would find out pretty quickly what's going on up here, and chill is the polar opposite. This actually happened in the hospital after my third delivery, when Teddy almost came out before we got there and flew into the doctor's arms in record timing (I don't know how anyone can be considered "chill" after they pushed a mini-watermelon out of their vagina and tore their butthole, but hey, I wasn't about to argue with the man who made sure we lived through the whole debacle). My doctor said to the nurse, while I relaxed with Teddy on my chest in my room, "I love how chill Brandi is." Well, dude, let me tell you something. I know how this thing goes the third time around, and you, my friend and doctor, have gotten me through each one safely. I trust you—I owe you a lot! Even in this modern day,

[12] Jewel, *Never Broken* (New York: Penguin Random House, 2015), XVIII.

birth is a high-risk game. People sadly don't always come out unscathed. I know, because my friend, who was the nurse helping catch my babies in the maternity ward of our hospital, witnesses beautiful life coming into the world—and sometimes tragedy. So, ya, I was laying in the chill zone, happy that my baby was alive and I was alive and I was basking in this breathtaking moment and in the miracle of this fickle life. Perspective. Gratitude.

Little did he know that I had spent that particular pregnancy being so NOT chill, chasing (let's be serious . . . waddling) after two very busy boys running around on the street all summer. And boy, I was so fucking happy to have like three free hours to eat a hamburger covered in gravy that someone else cooked for me in a quiet room with one new little babe to take care of, and that was all. I felt like the queen of fucking England that day, let me tell you!

Being content, and soaking in the present moment, can be one of the greatest tools and pleasures in our lives.

Flow in the river of life, lay back, feel the water around your body, and wonder in amazement how you got here and glory in the miracle that this river is holding you up because you trust the way in which it connects with every part of your body.

Say out loud three things you are grateful for at this very moment.

If we want to get really graphic here, let's talk about the flow of birthing babies! The baby moves slowly into position and its head sits on the cervix, slowly stretching it through time, and when you walk around, you can feel the constant pressure and think, *This thing must come out of me!* But it's all necessary to the process of preparing for birth or what happens . . . if you don't trust in the process and the baby needs to come out, the doctors book you for an induction and your body has to blast this baby out without the cervix being warmed up and ready for what is to come. It's something called a starburst tear—a star has five points. Enough said I think . . . it friggin' hurts. For a long, long time. I myself got to experience the birth that my body wasn't prepared for the first time around.

Birth is something we have very little control over, comparable to life. We have no control—just our perception of how much control we are in. When it comes to birth, everyone just hopes to make it through the ordeal safely. With my first child, I arrived with a birth plan and my doctor sloughed it aside. He said we were just going to make sure we all get out of this safely; that is his job and he would cut my butthole if he needed to. He didn't actually say that, but after the starburst tear and the birth, I got it. I really, really got it. After the fear of your baby's heart rate dropping and almost heading for an emergency C-section, yes, please cut it so we can all make it through this.

Birth really has a way of stripping it all away. No one is in control. You are there in the most momentous thing you will ever experience; you will weep tears of joy at the simple beauty of life. A moment of impact pulling you directly into the present, where lives hang in the balance.

My second child, however, was a birth I felt happening slowly. That morning I said, I think this is it . . . no rush. We will go on a walk as a family. Not ready. We will have spaghetti and have a bath and put Gus to bed. Not ready. Try to sleep. Ready! Hospital at 1 a.m. Not ready. 3 a.m., watch Jamie Oliver grill a cheeseburger, go ask the nurse for some food, eat toast, and bounce around on a ball while I watch my husband sleep in a chair, wishing he would just go pick me up a burger already. Not ready. 7 a.m.—ready! Now! No starburst tear this time around. My body was ready. It had time to prepare and stretch and room for birth to happen beautifully on its own.

For my third birth we had numerous nights of bags packed and ready to go to the hospital, only for the sun to come up and me to walk up our driveway and head back inside, annoyed I had been up since 1 a.m. Teddy likes to tease people. Until one night my nurse friend was over, and she's like, no way you are in labour; it's false again. She leaves and ten minutes later I am sprinting down the stairs hoping the baby doesn't fall out onto the carpet at the bottom. Teddy flew out into the doctor's arms at the hospital just in time.

The first birth had to be an induction because of gestational diabetes, making it high-risk—that was just something out of my realm of control. The reason I am telling you all these stories, and the point I am trying to make, is this: We are not in control, control is an illusion. We have the power of choice, and we have the power of who we want to be and what we want to say. Embrace those things that you can focus on and accept that the rest will happen the way it was supposed to.

As much as I say go with the flow, you also need to have structure in place in your life to be successful or happy. Being in a routine will add ease and grace to your day, allowing for fun and flow.

I know some of us are better at flow than others. But I think it is a muscle that you can stretch slowly, something you can get better at. Certainly children have taught me about going with the flow. I mean, I didn't really have a choice. My partner married an artist; he, too, has certainly learned to go with my creative flow. I am sure lucky to have him. Every day I am sure I surprise him with what new and exciting thing I am going to create and bring forth into this world. I always come out of my studio with all the vigour and gumption about the art world and community and the importance of creativity and all my students in my classes. To his credit, he doesn't always know exactly what I am talking about, and may sometimes struggle to keep up, but he has always supported me in everything I do.

So stretch your flow and find people who will flex and challenge your flow right alongside you in this life, for there can be nothing more beautiful than that.

Routine

The best way to tackle the day if you are a parent is to set a routine and stick with it. I promise it will work if you stick with it! Movement combined with fresh air is the most nurturing and beautiful thing you can gift yourself and your family. If you can't make it out, make a space in your home for moving. There are so many resources now: you can do yoga at home, you can dance at home, you can do cardio—no need for the gym. Or just go for a walk; just do it!

The next one is a gem: zones. Red, green, and yellow. You obviously want to stay in the green; yellow happens, but we can deal with it; red is, well, red means shit has hit the fan and there is no going back! This goes for all ages, and here's a checklist for every day with kids:

- Sleep and rest when you need
- Eat three meals and snacks (like, real food)
- Move your body
- Plan ahead

Seems a little too simple, but it's not, although it is, once you're in it. Then it will change and you will adjust little things here and there, but the checklist stays the same. Having these all included in your day, in your own unique routine, will keep you out of the red zone. Plan ahead, pack food, be on time, don't head to the store thirty minutes before nap time, don't stay up for the extra episode, you get me? It is never worth falling out of the zone, it really isn't! My BIGGEST and most useful TIP would have to be weaving—not actual weaving, but it is a really great visual—weaving in about your day. Another graceful way of multitasking.

Let's say you are trying to make dinner, but you haven't been giving your child attention for more than thirty minutes while you cleaned and they are at your feet (or, if you have a baby Teddy, they are emptying the garbage and pulling dirt out of the plant for your attention because they want to be fed, stinkers). What you NEED to do is weave over to the kids in between the tasks! Vacuum, then spend ten to fifteen minutes playing cars or reading books, then weave over to your next task. Do this all day—it WILL work. Everyone is happy, everyone is loved.

The routine for sleep and consistent bed/nap time is the most crucial structure for children because it allows you time for yourself, which we all need. Self-care is so overlooked. You must take care of yourself first before you can best take care of others; whatever that means to you, leave space and time for you: reading, having a nice long bath, running, creating, listening to music, meditation, just do you. AND, just a reminder, grocery shopping is not a break, showering is not a luxury (it is hygiene), a nap is not lazy, and you deserve time for you—you are worth it. Sleep, oh my gosh, SLEEP, if you can, try really effing hard to sleep; it is actually the most helpful tool of all to bring love and joy into your everyday life.

Stick to all of this and it will leave room for love and care for everyone, and bonus if you get the kids to bed on time tonight—you get to do whatever the fuck you want! Woot woot!

The best part of all of this, being at home with my family, is when they are small, like mine are, they think you are the absolute bee's knees. That is actually the coolest, because I know it won't always be this way. When people with older children tell me, "This is the best time of your life, appreciate it," I believe them! Your kids love and adore you, despite all of your quirks and flaws. You can literally throw a box on your head and it will be the most HILARIOUS thing they have ever seen!

All you have to do is show up and you've got them on a string, pulling them through the oncoming obstacles each day will present. They don't look at me and think, *When was the last time she washed her hair?* or *Was that the shirt she wore yesterday? Do those pants have a hole in the butt?* (Actually, they do notice that and wiggle their little fingers into the hole.) *What kind of dance moves are those?* No! They see me as their ringleader through this circus we call life. They have no clue that I have absolutely no extra cash to buy them the coolest toys (because instead of working, I have had the luxury of being here at home with them), because they don't need material things. Kids are paid with hugs, kisses, snuggles, smiles, play, and high fives. So yes, I am tired. Because some of my days I have to make a million things happen, I am on fire, mom of the year! But then there are other days . . . the days where not much at all happens, or that downright stink (eye-rubbing, hair-pulling hard). I have to accept that there are days when just being there for them is enough.

I am enough—my love, your love, is enough. May we celebrate it with all the love in our hearts.

Choose Your Own Adventure

Every morning you pull yourself off that mattress you *get to* choose your own adventure. You make a conscious decision to put a little mustard on it or have a ho-hum day.

There is no doubt that every day is filled with menial tasks, but they all add up to your life, your beautiful wonderful life that you have the opportunity to control. Your hands are always on the wheel—be aware of that, think it through, let it sink in.

Car wash, ughhh, I hate filling up with gas or washing my car. It's just one of those things. Now that I have three kids, loading them all up in full winter gear and heading to the car wash in -25 degrees Celsius seems like an effing nightmare—pass. But, alas, it must be done.

One day midyear of being locked in the house with my three children, the car wash was on the docket. So I decided to make up a "choose your own adventure day." Everything we did was a magical mystery adventure—not really . . . it was literally going to Walmart and the car wash. I just put a super-fun spin on things! The joy that poured out of my three boys was palpable, and I got more and more into it as we went on. The greatest part is that the car wash bay needed a code to get in; it just couldn't get any better. We had this secret passcode that I got from a wizard inside and when you put it in, the overhead door opens and lets you through. I have to say, this menial day was one for the books!

So, do you choose a magical adventure with wizards and secret codes or are you just semi-jazzed to be here?!

Perfection Is Overrated

> *"The whole process of mental adjustment and atonement can be summed up in one word: gratitude."*
>
> – Wallace D. Wattles

Let's talk about that weird folding and organizational trend that got the whole world's panties in a knot (no, not in a knot . . . folded) with all the methods. (Sorry, not trying to disregard who this has worked for; I'm sure it has changed some lives, it just didn't work for us.)

This approach makes people turn their whole houses upside down and organize it in one special way, because it is the "better" way. It will make your life better to fold your clothes like this and have separate fancy containers for your eggs. My eggs get plopped right into the shelf of the fridge; there is no way I am picking up every fucking egg and placing it gently into the fancy fridge egg container. Who has time for that?!

It eventually came out that some of those methods are impossible to maintain with children. NO FUCKING SHIT?! Basically, any semblance of anything is impossible to maintain with children. When and how can I wash my hair? There are some mysterious nuggets caught up in this semblance of a messy bun! AND NOW I can't fold a fucking tee shirt because I can't decide what method I'd like to use and at the end of the goddamned week, it's all on the floor anyway, so who really cares!?

Who CARES how they went in and if you colour-coded it, tri-folded, compartmentalized it? Let it go. Look around your house and your life and take on what YOU can do in a day. Kick back, play with your kids, watch that movie with your partner, write your book, read that series you meant to get to, write a song, or create something! A lot of days there are, I'm sure, half-eaten plates from the last meal and toys everywhere, but at least you spent that last bit of time playing hide-and-seek or talking on the phone your mom.

Let's face it, if I make it through the day with my three boys under six alive and fed, it's a win!

One human can only do so much, and let me tell you, it feels phenomenal letting it all go. If you like to have your eggs in a fancier-looking thingamabob, then you do you. But for me, it's putting on slippers and walking all over the crumbs, because the alternative is vacuuming literally four times a day with the stage my kids are at. But I CHOOSE to be the lava monster instead and throw the cushions all over the dirty floor and tickle and laugh and dance and make lasting memories. What am I trying to prove here? It all boils down to what you want to be remembered for, who you want to be, and what will make you die happy and somewhat content. Whatever it is, do it, because all we have is now.

Laundry

I do have a great laundry tip, however upset I am about my folding predicament! Laundry is something that just isn't going to fold itself, and I don't have a nanny. I like my job, but I choose to make it work from home. My epic laundry trick is to yell out as loud, and with as much gusto as I can, "HIDE AND GO SEEK!" I chase them up the stairs and start counting really loudly and slowly . . . I head to the laundry room to fold and tackle the eight loads I've washed for the week. (I always throw a load in in the morning after I get dressed before I head downstairs—routine and consistency are key.)

While I'm folding, the boys run with one another, finding the best spot, or fighting over who gets to hide with who. I put on music or an audiobook as a treat for myself, or just bask in the silence of the room and the monotonous task of just doing something with my hands. Occasionally, I put the shirt I'm folding down and run after and tickle them. They still love it, even if we've been doing this same thing for about five years now. Laundry in our house has become, well, not so bad!

It's really all about perspective. If I didn't have laundry to fold, we wouldn't have clothes to wear. The clothes that keep us warm, the clothes that are an expression of who we are, the clothes that snuggle my little babies to sleep at night. I want to treat the small task of laundry, which most of us have, with the utmost gratitude. Love your laundry. You're lucky to have it.

What is one of your main complaints and how can you look at it from another perspective and make it, well, not so bad!?

Connection

Today I got to see my mom's sisters for the first time in two years. Is it two years?! Pretty much. Wow, time just ticks on by. It is so lovely to see them and spend time with them. It is like getting a little piece of my mom back again in tiny little bits and pieces. I hear it in the stories they tell and the sound of their laughter. They were so close and came from a family of thirteen children. They looked out for one another. Heck, I even think my mom saved her brother from drowning once. Needless to say, they were all closer than close on so many levels—the older children raised the middle and the middle children raised the babies. That is what my Grandma Kay told me once.

My aunts and uncles were staying at a campsite outside of town and I had to drive back to put Teddy down for a nap. Lo and behold, "Blue Eyes Crying in the Rain" came on the radio. The very song that had been sung at every family gathering, and the song my Grandma Kay requested every time a guitar came out. I can even hear her singing it right now. It is the song we sang to our mom the last night we got to be with her. The most vibrant and vivid, sorrowful moments of my life. So, THE song came on the radio right after seeing my aunties—you cannot tell me that this universe is not magical and connected on many more levels than we are aware of. We just need to be open and ready to hold and feel each moment and take them with grace. There is a lesson to be held in each one. Moving us all forward, with our loved ones carrying us along in the wind.

Is there someone you'd like to reconnect with whom you haven't been able to in a while? Reach out, send them a message. They are most likely feeling the same way you are.

We all need human connection, support, and love. Even if you think I am off-my-rocker crazy here, with all my babbling about songs and signs and whatnot. Don't you think there is something to be said about belief in something and how that makes you feel? Whatever you do believe, divine or not, if it makes you feel less lonely and genuinely inspired, and fires and feeds your spirit and soul, that has just got to be good for something. We genuinely need connection. We need meaning and purpose—it is the key to a healthy and balanced life. We can't do it all alone, and we shouldn't.

Don't Try to Take the World on Alone, It Takes a Village

Our family models have changed so drastically, with everyone having their own home and their own space. Their own phone, computer, and room, with no environmental stimulation or organic interaction. THIS IS A REAL PROBLEM. Especially in North American culture. Raising a family used to look a lot different than it does now. But we are expected to take on parenting alone, and it is just not possible. It takes a village. Your children need to learn from others; they need connection with people other than you. I know, I know, we have been through a confusing and new time, and every situation is unique. But we cannot be our best selves, and they cannot grow and develop to their fullest potential, without outside exposure.

If you don't live near immediate family, make friends and connections; friends are, after all, the family you choose. Take breaks. Ask for help. Host family dinners. Make an effort. For yourself and your children.

If we have anything to take away from the two years of the pandemic, it is how important that connection was to our well-being, purpose, and overall happiness.

What is something you took for granted before?

Now, how will you try to move forward with that knowledge?

Accept the Lows & Rest

Lows. Of course there are lows. Without a low there would be no high—there is always a balance. Although, if you are a parent, or if you are part of a team or run your own business, there is no option but to show up. Your children need you, in all of your forms—and that is a reality they should see and accept: we are not all perfect all the time.

I remember being so sick and tired when I was pregnant with my third child, and all I could do was lie on the floor for three months in the living room, doing my best to keep everyone fed and in their daily routines. Following each task I would collapse on the rug, nauseous. As it turns out, kids kind of love you no matter what form you greet them with—they are cool like that! They loved that I was finally available to meet them at their level instead of running around all the time, cooking, cleaning, running my in-home business. They wrestled on top of me, gave me a million kisses and hugs and snuggles, and we watched movies and had living room picnics.

We did the best with what life had presented to us at that moment. Now I can look back at that time, not as a mom who was defeated, but as a mom who did her very best with what she had. I soaked in all of the snuggles and thought, *How awesome and how resilient are my children?!*

The best way to conquer, endure, or accept the lows is to notice and be mindful of when you typically go into a low and prepare in advance. Book a day off, or try to get a lot of work done before it hits, or get a grandparent or friend to take your kids. For women, it is a bit like hormonal clockwork. Or if you know there is a huge project you've been working on and another one following that, you have to leave time for yourself to recharge.

When I think about it, what will my children care about more: that I spent that extra ten minutes at bedtime finding Waldo and the Wizard in their favourite *Where's Waldo?* book or that I worked extra that night on a painting or my podcast? They want ten minutes of my time. Ten, out of my whole evening. They don't give a shit about all the stuff I strive for; they just want me. I have drive—great—I have passion—good—they will see that, and it will empower them to do the same in their lives. But those qualities do not define me. What defines me is my ability to show up, show up for the people I love in every way I possibly can. That is what keeps my heart beating until the very end. If I can inspire others to do the same, live with more compassion and love, that feeds my soul along that journey beautifully. What a journey it will be!

I will never stop being creative. No one can ever take that away; it is a part of me, but just one part. Everything I touch has a little bit of that creative magic thrown in, and it all leads up to this moment. I am just aware that it can change and evolve and mould with me over time, and that is OKAY with me. It just maybe didn't turn out the way everyone said it should. Period.

The Disney Pixar movie *Soul* has this great quote after their main character, Joe, the musician, finally gets the big gig he thought would change his whole life and was confused when he didn't feel THAT different after he hit one of his lifetime goals. It's one that I will just never forget:

DORTHEA: What's wrong, teach?

JOE: It's just I've been waiting on this day for my entire life. I thought I'd feel different.

DORTHEA: I heard this story about a fish. He swims up to this older fish and says, "I'm trying to find this thing they call the ocean." "The ocean?" says the older fish, "That's what you're in right now." "This?" says the younger fish, "This is water. What I want is the ocean."[13]

That's the thing about goals: they have a tendency to be a cloud over your head blocking your sunshine or not living up to your expectations. Instead imagine the life you see for yourself and work little by little the best you can every single day.

It's All about the Journey

We are so caught up in getting to the places we want and where we "think" we need to be we forget that we have to be present in our everyday lives.

I have already mentioned my 2011 painting residency in France (where I mostly indulged in red wine, cheese, and bread, and that is okay). My dad decided he would meet me in Paris and we would pop down to Italy by train. My dad is quite the character and is such a cool dude in so many ways, very unique and not afraid to be anyone but himself. It is a pretty neat thing to be raised by a special person like that.

Our third stop in Italy was Verona, and by that time we were all a bit tired—turns out you should not try to fit four cities by train into one week. On our first night in picturesque Verona, we were exploring the city by foot—it is such a neat spot with cobblestone streets and shop fronts and lovely places to eat and drink around every corner on the way to the city centre.

That evening, there was no real place to go, except for dinner. EATING was number one in my mind (I live to eat). My life basically revolves around when I get to my next meal and how exquisite it is going to be. I firmly believe that if something hits your lips, it better be the best

[13] *Soul*, Disney+, directed by Pete Docter and Kemp Powers (Emeryville, CA: Pixar Animation Studios, 2020).

fucking thing that you could have imagined or what's the point? This level of snobbery as a parent has been a bit more challenging with the basic lack of time and need for sustenance to keep the old fuel tank full to keep chasing after Teddy. OKAY, so you get how much I like food.

Back to the streets of Verona . . . I was on the brink of HANGRY—a don't-fuck-with-me kind of mood! Which, as I just mentioned, is never the best place for anyone to be. We were strolling down the wide and sparkly streets of Verona. My Dad was literally, and by literally, I mean *literally*, taking a picture of every friggin' window display (what he planned to do with these, I have no idea, but he was on a goddamn mission). It was taking a lifetime to get even one block covered.

Finally, I had had enough and walked right up to him, took his camera right out of his hands and proceeded to stride off in a fit of hungry anger, a steaming bowl of red wine risotto with freshly grated parm on top in mind. Smug with success, I then stopped because I realized my dad was not astride beside me—what now? I turned around to look back, only to find he had pulled a spare camera from the side pocket of his cargo pants. I was enraged, but I could not ignore how funny it all was! We laughed so hard then, and we still tell this story about my dad and his many cargo pockets and what they hold. He refuses to change or care what anyone thinks, and it's a glorious quality to have. He ties his Bluetooth speaker to his belt and strides through life rockin' to CKUA radio wherever he goes and has decided that he should finally grow himself a ponytail. I love him so much.

It is easy to get so caught up in the anger and the situations where all you see is red and you have lost absolutely all patience. I get it—it is SO MUCH easier to LOSE YOUR SHIT, and that is our knee-jerk reaction! Especially when it comes to our immediate family. But this is something you can learn to adjust, take hold of, and master over time. By simply taking pause and walking away to get some space and collect yourself, or take some wind, like I tell my son Finn (who has a similar temperament to mine). Then move forward. What do we gain from losing our shit? Not much, but a nice heavy round of guilt and shame that follows.

Why not laugh instead, when you can? My husband took a hilarious video the other morning. My son found my "personal massager" in my bathroom drawer, turned it on and was combing his hair with it. We rewatched it and all you can hear is me screaming in the background about the whole box of cereal Teddy had poured in his toy sink full of water and what a waste it was. Being an asshat is not necessary, especially when it plays to the background of your kid combing his hair with your you-know-what.

Laugh. It feels better. After all, it's all about the journey.

My husband also said I should definitely mention in this book how handsome he is. My husband is soooooo handsome, it's hard to get anything done when he's around. He is so handsome that if he got a dollar for every time someone told me I had a handsome husband I would be a millionaire.

Is there a story you can think of where you just had to laugh, even though you were mad?

Be Here

Be here. In the present moment: we must have the conscious ability to recognize and accept what we CAN and CANNOT control.

Wallace D. Wattles. Not only do I love to say his name—"Wallace D. Wattles"—but I really love how his book, written in the 1800s, still resonates in this current time. It is a bit of a religious book, but, like I mentioned before, everyone has their own unique god, universe, beliefs, rituals, prayers, and that is okay. Wattles's book is titled *The Science of Getting Rich*. Jen Sincero recommended this read in the back of her *You*

Are a Badass book. I decided to give it a go because if you haven't figured out already, I am a bit of a Jen S. fan! But I really connected with Wallace's core message. He speaks of using your energy as attraction and to focus it all on that and forget all the rest of the crap we worry about in a day. Take it all in as it comes—that is what we are in control of. Wattles states:

> *"You cannot act in the past. It is essential to the clearness of your mental vision that you dismiss the past from your mind. You cannot act in the future because the future is not here yet. And you cannot tell how you will want to act in any future contingency until that contingency has arrived."*[14]

Stop worrying about what you're supposed to be doing and just have faith. Trust that what you are doing in this moment of this very day is a small step toward where you are meant to be. Imagine you are floating in the calm waters of a river, feeling the light eddies flow around you, lightly lifting you up. You flow with the river to stay buoyant, trusting that the water will support your body and carry you where you need to be. Now, imagine if you don't trust the flow and you stiffen up, fight the flow . . . you sink, you flounder, you eventually will tire and drown. It takes a lot less energy to allow the river of life to elevate you and feel comfort that what is, is what was meant to be. Know that there will be trying times, and know that there will be beautiful times, and know that they both exist for different reasons. Observe them, and see how you can learn and grow from them. Pause, breathe, listen to the world around you. Observe the simplicity in the way things exist around you; it really is quite phenomenal when you think about it.

---

[14] Wallace D. Wattles, *The Science of Getting Rich* (CreateSpace Independent Publishing Platform, 2017), 74.

I imagine, like most things, this is something you have to consciously work at and integrate and weave into your life's daily motions. It is stretching your mind like an elastic, slowly and slowly, minute by minute, so it doesn't snap back or break. You are expanding the elasticity of your mindset, and this needs to be practised regularly for it to work—work out your consciousness the same way you work out your body.

I was recently interviewed by a spiritualish (that's a word, no?) woman for her podcast, and she said she was extremely interested in the science behind the mind. She proceeded to tell me that as soon as we open our eyes in the morning, our brains (comparably to a computer) take in over 10 billion bits of information all at once. I found this fact incredibly surprising and almost unbelievable. It made me realize we must apply continuous effort to master our focus, and the more we work on our focus muscles, the more it becomes a habit, and the muscles get bigger and are ever-expanding. In order for your brain to not be overwhelmed, it filters things through. How powerful it would be to control our filter. We would be unstoppable.

My favourite part about bringing consciousness to my day is when I pause to notice the expression on my baby's face as I toss him in the air, when I close my eyes to take in the sound of his laughter, when I feel his plump little body as I squeeze him into me for a big hug. The way his soft cheek feels on mine, his smell and cotton candy–like wisps of hair grazing my lips as I place a kiss on his warm head.

I find when I'm overwhelmed—even on the best of days this happens—lack of sleep or bad news can really throw me off track. It crashes down on me like a ton of anxious bricks. Can coffee fix this? No. It all gets away from me: *Wow, look at my house—what a mess. Oh my goodness, all those emails . . . wait, I need to do my banking. Why is my traffic so low for my business? Shoot, the baby is in the toilet. How can I make all this work? What am I even doing? How can I hit all my career goals and still be a good parent?*

This list of worries is a bottomless pit I try to avoid; it is a lurking void, threatening to suck you in at your weaker moments. My heartbeat increases and I can feel the blood rushing to my ears and my chest tightens. Then I remember: *Breathe, always breathe. What does that breath sound like, feel like? I notice my lungs filling and my ribs making way for the air flowing in and out through my nose. Good, focused again. Now, what can I control right now in this very moment, priority number one: get Teddy out of the toilet; we'll figure the rest out later.*

Take a few deep breaths and embrace the fact that the world inevitably and always will be out of your control, and the only thing YOU or I can do is flow in the breeze of this wonderous wind of the very moment you are in. Taking in the awe and wonder of the ever-changing and evolving gusts breezing through our minds and bodies. Be in control of your filter. What can you control? Your perspective and the way you perceive the world around you.

The precious part of being present is the little things you enjoy that you somehow missed before, as if you were on autopilot. My ultimate meditation is when I put my baby down for a nap and I sit in the dark for ten minutes with a sound machine on while he becomes heavy and sleepy in my arms. It is a true gift of time, my mid-day meditation. I think I will keep doing this even after my children all grow, savouring my afternoon tea and my time to myself. It is a treat and a break in my chaotic day at home.

List your top ways to rest and be mindful; here are mine:

- Meditation
- Yoga
- A warm bath

- Quiet time (yes, everyone needs it, even adults)
- Nursing my baby (this one I will miss)—a dark room with my tiny little being that was once inside of me, one of the most beautiful wonders of this life, a level of connection that one cannot begin to describe; it is a feeling, a wonder, a gift.
-
-
-
-
-

Be Prepared or Unprepared for the Unexpected

That is correct, so intrinsically correct I can't even begin! Things don't always go your way; they never will go exactly as you plan. In fact, they tend to go so ass-backwards, we get thrown for a loop daily!

On a chilly April morning I found myself looking out to a fresh blanket of snow on the ground. I thought, *Shit, I guess we aren't having that picnic at the park we just talked sweetly about in my bed. Hmmm . . . that sucks.* But there comes Finn barrelling down the stairs. "Mom, there's snow! Did you see that snow all over the ground, Mom!?" Ya, dude, hard to miss. Sorry we can't go to the park for our picnic. He literally didn't even hear me; he began digging in the closet for his snow pants that I had washed and so ignorantly put away for the season. "Mom, do up my zipper! Where are my mitts? I'll need a toque! MOM, WHERE'S MY TOUQUE?!"

I darn well needed this. There was a lesson right there shouting at me in the face. HEY, BRANDI, things don't always go your way—or, in reality, the way you feel they should. When you think about this in the grand scheme of things, has anything ever gone "the way it should?" NO. Why? Because there is no perfect way. Things can turn out perfectly, but they are rarely planned.

Don't get me wrong—it is nice to plan and prepare. That always helps, especially when dealing with balancing your family. However, I am a big dreamer, and I have some grandiose plans, like, all the time! A few of my plans have not panned out. I cried. I was angry. I was discouraged. But with all of my heart I looked for the lesson. I tried so hard to keep finding that silver lining. And let me tell you, it's there. Have faith. There is a reason for each failure . . . that's the wrong word. There is a lesson: it really is NOT a failure. Sit back, reflect on what didn't maybe go as smoothly as it could, put one foot in front of the other, and step forward. Maybe that thing didn't work because you just were not ready, and next time you will be. You will be ready with bells on and take it in stride with confidence. And maybe, just maybe, realize that THAT wasn't for you—now you know, and now you can pour all your time and energy into something special.

Be open to flowing with the river instead of walking upstream, constantly fighting the current. Pull out your snow pants and go play in the snow, because gosh darn it, it's April and that snow will not be here in an hour—THIS IS YOUR LAST SNOWMAN that you get to build this year, enjoy it. Love this life, love yourself, and it will all come back to you tenfold!

Time has a way of escaping our grasp day to day. Before we know it our own children are grown and we start the beautiful journey of becoming grandparents. More recently I have been much more interested in hearing the stories from aunts, uncles, grandparents, and other more experienced parents than myself. This is how we pass down our knowledge and experiences, through storytelling. There is something so peaceful about asking the perfect question and having someone tell you a story about their life experience. There is always something to enjoy, and there is always something to learn. Never stop learning. Never stop growing and expanding yourself and stretching your mind.

Take a Lesson from Your Elders

One of the most beautiful things you can do is spend time with people who are older than you. They have a lot to offer. They have seen things and lived through much more than we can even fathom. Take time to sit, ask them questions, and listen to the answers. There is always something so rewarding and rich about connecting with not only people who are older and more experienced than you, but also with the ones who are related to you and who love you. They are literally the reason you are here, today, right now. You can learn something interesting about your family's history or find value and knowledge to take away from each conversation. As we know, time is always passing, and that person and their stories and their lifetime of experiences will go with them. Pick up the phone and call your grandma while she is still around.

One particular lesson and one particular trip I will never forget was with my mother going to visit my grandpa the week before he died. I wasn't quite sure what was going through my mom's head on the way to see him, and she didn't say. Only on occasion did she open up to me on these long drives, and I knew better than to ask after a lifetime of "mind your own business" retorts. She just quietly smoked in silence the whole way as she drove. I decided to lay my head down to sleep on the pillow she packed in the car. Her pillow, filled with goose down, crunchy and smelling of her choice perfume and cigarettes.

This was our routine on our trips. She drove, I slept. Sometimes she would take me in the car to the bridge that crossed the Saskatchewan River, just to drive. It was one of the things she just loved to do. Ashing her cigarette out the car window in a way that only she did. On this trip she contemplated in silence. I slept. I wonder now what was going on in her head, knowing this was the last time she would ever see or speak to her father.

I don't know a lot about my grandpa. What I do know has been passed down through tall-tale fishing stories. I do have a few memories of my own: him in the pink plush carpeted living room with the pink velvet couch and THE chair, HIS chair. I remember the green fabric footstool he set his calloused feet upon, with its dark mahogany legs. The stool and chair that was were only his, and that footstool held his jar of seasoned peanuts that was strictly off limits (but I always snuck some when no one was looking). It was easy to get lost amongst the sea of cousins and the hustle and bustle of over fifty people stuffed in one small home over the holidays.

I remember being there alone in that house with a black-and-white television that didn't work, or at least with nothing worth watching on the one channel. I remember not wanting to venture into the scary depths of the odd-smelling basement. The damp, dark unfinished basement that played host to the pinball machine, the one interesting piece of entertainment this quiet home held for me. I always found myself in this unfortunate predicament, risking being eaten by a monster in the basement or playing on the pinball machine. I remember also staring at a glass case built into the wall, which held my grandparents' wedding cake, wondering how I could get behind that glass to eat the cake. It is so strange the small bits of memories, smells, and sounds we take with us from our childhood, and why.

So, there we were, my mother and I on a summer day, floating along the quiet highway that vined its way through the endless fields of wheat swaying in the wind. As we drove, the hours stretched on. Finally, we arrived in northern Saskatchewan at my grandpa's trailer. We walked up the black steel steps into the dark to find him, his frail body curled up on the small daybed that could also be flipped into a table. As we sat in the uncomfortable stuffiness of the mobile home, we waited. To his great storyteller legacy, he did not disappoint, launching right into one of his epic fish stories about the five of diamonds, of course. As I sat there, I couldn't help but think of how it reminded me of the way my mom and her siblings tell a story and who this talent so clearly came from. I don't think he knew who I was exactly, but that didn't stop him.

However, seeing a young person triggered something beyond the tall tales of his fishing ventures. Lying there, finding me with his dark almond eyes that match my mother's and my own. He just kept pausing and looking over at me. Finally making this phone-typing motion with his hands. I knew what he meant and will never forget it, a small but momentous gesture: "those kids" don't see their lives that are right in front of them. This man who had very few breaths left and had lived a full life pointed out the central problem for humankind: we cannot live our true lives through a device; this is not living. Take it from a man who really lived, who came into the world in the dirty '30s, survived a world war, and helped manage thirteen children into adulthood. A man who lived, passing on in the face of death, a gift for me to share with you right now in this very moment in time: Live. Here. Now. Through your physical body, live. Because here is my grandfather's advice to me when he was on the steps of death's door—what he saw our generation doing with our hands is his interpretation of not living. We are missing out on moments of authentic connection.

Pick a time of day that you can put your devices aside and just talk to one another; make it a solid rule, no compromises, and stick to it. Our favourite time to do this is dinnertime.

The Day That Instagram Died

"Bye-bye, Instagram Live, drove my Chevy to the levee but the levee was dry," sung to the tune of "American Pie." It was such a weird day. But my reaction was unexpected, like, good, I hope it dies; then I can get back to living my life. In the same breath, I love all my friends and connections and, of course, my business depends on Instagram, hard. However, I felt relieved; a weight had been lifted. I played with my kids, worked in the garden, enjoyed the menial yet beautiful tasks of the day as opposed to having to capture and share them.

It was an eye-opener to see how dependent I was on a device. Of course, these are all things I know, all things I have known for a while, all things I preach to my partner when he has his head down mindlessly scrolling. However, it is one thing to say things and another to put them into practice. It was a slap in the face, a cold bucket of water dumped on my reality. WAKE THE FUCK UP. Come out of the device coma. We fear a zombie apocalypse, but maybe we are in one, where we all walk around in a semi-alive trance. Sorry, I served a bit of a shit sandwich there, but seriously, what is happening? Cue Old Man voice: "When I was a kid, we didn't have phones; we walked five miles to get our mail."

We need to focus on what is real, what is in front of us, or we will be in our deathbeds wondering what the fuck was it all for?! How often do we slough off our children for that web video? Or sit with our friends or partner, glued to our phone? I get it, that it is the way we literally communicate in the modern day, but it is not healthy by any means. Stop, just stop. Look people in the eye, tell them how much you love them, hold them, feel them, and observe your surroundings. Engage, play, embrace, laugh—these are normal things we should be doing every day, but they are slowly becoming out of the norm. There is no going back; this is all here to stay and we have to adjust and create balance, because it is healthy for our minds and bodies to do so. All I am preaching is to be more conscious of your device use.

I can get so caught up running all the platforms for my business, it seems like I am running from one to the next, and I can never get off, even if I want to. I am an artist and find that I spend about 80 percent of my art time on my computer and phone instead of practising the magical act I have been gifted with: creation. It hurts my heart to put my creative energy on hold. I am sure I am not the only one. Can you relate to this?

Reflect and reevaluate how you spend your time and when you can incorporate connection, not only to your loved ones but also to yourself.

Connecting Organically

There has been no greater time where we have to consciously choose to disconnect. There is no doubt the world is changing rapidly before our eyes. There are positives and negatives to this as we navigate through it all. We will greet this with grace and flow, taking it in minute by minute. I do, however, need to stress to you one thing that we need to pay attention to constantly, and that is organic connection. We have to hang on to our humanity the best we can. No amount of online chatting can replace staring into your child's eyes and witnessing their uninhibited view of the world, their brand-new world. Nothing can replace an embrace from a lover or how you intimately interact with one another.

I'm sure you've all heard this before, but put down your phone. Phones and devices are literally made to keep you engaged like an addict.

I am a big DND (do not disturb) person, even before my business relied on my device. THERE IS NO WAY I could function through a day having my notifications on. I literally would be working all twenty-four hours, getting dings every three minutes. This was an awesome habit to get into; I get back to others on my time. Time when my children are otherwise engaged or asleep. My husband needs to be reminded constantly; admittedly this makes my blood boil. I know he tries, but he is just really unable to ignore his phone.

I know some people are unable to have the luxury of turning DND on. If this is you, I ask you to book designated times into your day so you can unplug and connect organically, not only with others around you but with yourself. Take that glorious bubble bath in silence. Run or walk in the woods and listen to the amazing world around you. There is no better sound than trees rustling and birds chirping.

Are you getting enough organic connection?

If not, how can you fit more into your week?

The Simple Things

Every Saturday morning my mom would blast the stereo in the living room, attempting to motivate us to clean the house with her. It was actually always fun, and I often found these are the most memorable moments of my childhood of us hanging out as a family in the living room and not actually cleaning. For the most part, my brother would put tape on a balled-up sock and we would play sock hockey with our hands. It was a perfect game and distraction in our '70s-style, small drop-down living room. It was also about the only time I got to spend with my cool four-years-older brother.

Remember a time when, you know, we all just organically hung out, listening to music or making up games? We now have to make a conscious effort today to connect. There are just literally too many distractions; it is unhealthy, without a doubt. Again, I know I sound like an old man ("Remember the good old days? I had to walk eight miles, uphill, in a snowstorm to get to school.") But it's true—we have so much more, but so much less at the same time.

I am consciously aware of the fact that when I spend too much time working on my computer, I am a raging beast afterward. Or when my littles play video games for too long, there is an inevitable breakdown. It's because we need fresh air, we need the sun, we need to connect to other humans. If anything, we've learned from recent events in this world that we desire, long for, and crave embrace and social interaction. Connection is a necessity of living.

When to Throw in the Towel

Being at home every day with your wild things is a journey, with several obstacles, and just as many thrilling sights. At this very moment of this very evening, I have put Teddy back to bed nine times—parenting is not for the faint of heart. Someone once asked me, "Well, isn't this what you signed up for?" No, not really . . . no one expects parenting to be the way it is; no one can forewarn you. Parenting, while difficult to say the least, can be the most exhilarating and rewarding ride in this life. It can also kick you while you are down, really hard.

Breathe it in, let it out, let it go . . . tomorrow they will grow and change and be a more evolved humans than they were the day before and so will you. They greet each and every day with an open mind and a willingness to learn and explore. That in itself is pretty darn cool. Before we know it, they will be yelling at us to get out of their rooms instead of begging us to sing that extra lullaby for the ninth fucking time. Perspective. Know that this, and every other moment, shall pass, and we need to relish in all the special parts.

Know your limits and know when to throw in the towel. Example: I am going to stop, cutting this chapter short, and go put Teddy back to bed AGAIN! Hit the pillow myself, for I may just start weeping, mentally exhausted. We all know our own limits.

What are the signs for you when you should just call it a day?

Alone Time

Fast-forwarding you right into this very moment as I sit reflecting on this crazy year I've just had, I want to tell you why I am here right now, ALONE, and why I started talking about self-care. I realized I needed a recharge. I was resenting my partner and my children, which made me feel sick to my stomach. I am in no way complaining. I am grateful to be alive and have a healthy, special family in the life we've created for ourselves. But it had gotten to the point where I had not a lot left to give. Then I really questioned why I felt this way. I realized that I hadn't been alone for twenty-four hours in three years. This Mama needed some me time! So here I sit at a hotel I can barely afford eating a fancy-ass dinner at a fancy-ass place!

As soon as I booked myself the first night away from my little pod in three years, I felt a weight being lifted off my shoulders. I was looking forward to reconnecting to myself again. You know what? I deserved it. Seven years of nursing three babies and making sure they safely made it through the day is a LOT for anyone. By safely, I mean no one gravely injuring themselves, which you can't quite fathom until you are a parent yourself, the fear. With my three boys there have been a few questionable situations that I am embarrassed to mention. Finn put broken glass in his mouth once. Teddy likes to climb to heart-stopping heights and jets out onto the road into full traffic on his strider bike, to the point where his grandpa can no longer bring his bike with them on their walks. This is judgement-free space here, right? I mean three outnumbers two, and it certainly outnumbers one, and that is me on a lot of days.

The morning before I left, I came downstairs and Teddy had dumped out the whole bin of tortilla chips all over the living room carpet and furniture—just, like, fuck me—and then pooped on the floor a bit, which Finn got on his hands and attempted to wipe off on his pants. Teddy waddles over and says, "Oh, mom, my poop." Ya, we know, who else would have dropped a poop nugget on the kitchen floor? I mean that is a greaaaaaaat start to a day, and it literally is how most mornings begin for our family. What was I doing while this took place, you ask? Putting on clothes and brushing my teeth, which takes about seven minutes, and shit always hits the fan—sometimes literally.

There, now at least you can picture the reason why I booked a hotel and am leaving just for a bit. But it is not just to recharge. I have been wanting more than fifteen-minute intervals to write to you here. I really would love to finish this little ditty, and I can tell you right now I am thoroughly enjoying laughing to myself in this public space while solely sipping on prosecco. I don't really drink, but on this rare occasion it is a treat. I know my limits. Accomplishing what I have calls for a celebration and a loud declaration that everyone deserves— you deserve—a moment, or many moments, dedicated to just ourselves.

Ways you can recognize the signs of burnout:

- You can't stand work.
- You can't stand other humans.
- You can't stand the humans you love.
- You can't stand yourself.
- You haven't showered for a while, and so on and so forth.

Take a fucking break—you deserve it!

On the day I took my trip away from home. . . . The still, deep dark before the dawn and the haunting panic sets in: What day is it? Where are we going? What is on the agenda for the morning? Who is going to school? Who is going to work? Are we picking up groceries afterward? It all crashed down on my chest in a heavy rush of anxious thought.

Until I note that I am not at home, this is not my bed, and my baby has not swiftly woken me up before dawn. I have risen on my own. The heaviness falls away like tiny bits of sand crumbling off after you've been buried under a pile of it at the beach.

I rise out of the soft, crisp white hotel sheets. Make a tea and sit at the desk, relishing the moment of slowly bobbing the tea bag up and down by the string in the steaming cup of hot water, while I appreciate the beauty of this simple task.

It has been eighteen hours since I left them. The world is quiet and moves along at a calm, natural pace, one to which I am no longer accustomed. The Saskatchewan River flows with beautiful hexagon-shaped ice pieces floating along it. The rise peeks on the horizon the way the sun does in the prairies for miles and miles. There is no way to describe it that will make you appreciate its powerful presence. The only way to know is to experience its vastness yourself.

It has been eighteen hours since I left them. It is a balance that was necessary, a reflection that was called for, a desperate attempt to grasp onto the pieces of myself. Feel like me again, if only for a few hours, reconnect to the quiet, reconnect to control, reconnect to the simple joys, and bask in the small moments. Necessary in the way that three lives I helped create are attached to my very being. I am their safe haven, ruling mistress, adventure guide, and soft, squishy spot to lay their heads. A tall order to fill, a role that demands constant vigilance and takes the mental capacity and patience of a dictator running a small country.

It has been eighteen hours since I left them. I miss my baby's body on mine as he nurses right before the sun rises every morning, and I relish the moment because this, like so many, will never be the same. Our inevitable truth is that our babies will grow old and need us in different ways. But this way was the grandest attachment one will ever experience to another human soul. The contentment that falls over both mother and child in the quiet comfort of our bed right before dawn.

Shit Happens, It Just Does

About that solo trip to recharge . . . it has been twenty hours since I left them. And two hours since I was writing poetically by the river in my hotel room. One hour since I found out my tire was flat on our fancy car my husband was so hesitant to let me drive on this trip. I call it the COVID car, because it would have never been purchased had I not had a temporary lapse in judgement, like fuck it, life is short, get that car of your dreams!

This afternoon I envisioned myself quietly, slowly plucking away at the letters on my keyboard, deep in thought, sipping slowly on a lovely beverage, pausing only to contemplate my next profound thought.

WELLLLL, SHIT HAPPENS. Like, all the time, shit happens. I was driving his car, about to head to said café, when I thought, *Hmmmm, something just doesn't feel quite right.* Bam! His car flashes at me: LOW INFLATION. "Fuuuuuuuuuuuuuck," I moaned to myself. No no no no no, this just can't be happening. Of course this is happening, yep, fuck. I map out the closest tire shop. Yep, confirmed damaged tire. Cool.

"We can fix it for you tomorrow."

"Ummm, ya, I need to be home to my kids in four hours and we live two hours away."

"Sorry, ma'am, I just don't see that happening for you."

GREAT. Map out the next tire location, Trail Tires Auto Centres in Edmonton. At this point I am crying, because all my emotions live right below my skin, always bubbling up and pouring over for everyone to witness.

I walk into Trail Tires and explain to them my untimely predicament. I can tell they have no room for me at all, but they show me kindness, regardless. There are kind humans amongst us. And although I am now plucking my keys while I witness the hustle and bustle of the employees flinging tires about and the smell of gas and oil lingering in the air, I cannot be angry or upset. Shit happens. There are kind people to help you when said shit happens. Things will not always go to plan. That is why I always say "don't overthink it," because there is just no way to predict the future. No matter the planning that goes into anything, a wrench could be thrown in, a wrench that pops your tire.

It is funny, I had packed some art prints to give away while I was here and I left my hotel room with only one left, thinking, *Hmmm what will I do with this last one? I'll find out, I guess.* Well, a very nice man will have a lovely gift for his wife when he goes home from work today.

You Get to Choose Where You Want the Shit to Happen

If those twenty-four hours on this overnight trip away from my family taught me anything, it is this: you get to choose WHERE you want the shit to happen.

No matter where you lay your head gently on your pillow every evening, your day will be preceded with a classic mixture of crazy-good, mediocre moments, magical clarity, and/or terribly bad events. You need to choose where you are happiest having all these things happen to you. Because as I drive my way home, biting my nails through the bustling traffic of the city I escaped to from my family, I am longing for the expected moments of my day-to-day life with my children.

Yes, I took a break because I definitely needed it. But you just forget that the grass is always greener in the context of your mind. You forget that no matter where you are and what you are doing, there are going to be little blips along the way and times where you rub the sides of your temples in frustration. Even if you see yourself on holiday sipping a cocktail on the beach, you still need to brave the airport, the flight, the taxi ride, and check in and recover from jet lag. Everything comes with a whole lotta mental and physical baggage.

This trip was the perfect reminder that there are a few perks to other places, but the grass is most definitely not greener than where I get to roll through the motions of the day with the people I love the most in the world.

Leaving was honestly booked in haste after I was accidentally clocked in the face by a flying yo-yo and had a fully fuelled breakdown in the laundry room following the incident. It was time to take a little time for myself and be away from my children for at least twenty-four hours.

Hour twenty-eight, I am home. After a long journey—more emotional than expected, and it didn't quite go off without a hitch like I hoped. Quite the opposite, in fact. My sister purchased the Brandi Carlile audiobook for me a few months before my trip. I plugged it in while I had a few hours to listen to something kid-free. My sister did buy it for me with a warning attached—a warning to be ready to cry—and I don't think I took her seriously enough, because I am still reeling from the impact of the book.

I don't know if I can fully go into the significance of Brandi Carlile in my life. Though I obviously don't know her, I have always felt this odd connection. I found one of her songs randomly in 2006 by accidentally downloading it on iTunes I think. (Those were the old days, when we didn't have unlimited music at our fingertips, before touchscreens, right before the iPod and Facebook changed everything.) Anyway, I had accidentally downloaded her song because my name is Brandi and my partner's (now husband's) name is Carly, and I had typed that into the search bar and her name was there, and I thought, wow, neat. There was no coming back, I was hooked.

Later I found her full album and it was a lifelong love of her flowing through our car speakers on every road trip from there on out. If you don't know who Brandi is, I highly suggest you find out. She bares her soul bravely in her book while singing her way through her life's story chronologically. When Brandi and twins Phillip John and Timothy Jay Hanseroth played at the Winspear Centre with the Edmonton Orchestra, we went to both concerts. They were jaw-dropping performances and experiences I will always hold dear. My mom made it to the first but was too sick to make it the following year's performance. At the second performance at that theatre I found a dime on the floor. This doesn't mean anything to you yet, but it meant everything to me, and you will learn why later.

It is really hard to explain this, mostly because it really isn't my story or my journey to share. But I know my mom connected deeply to Brandi in ways that I will never truly know because we are two very different people. My mom resonated with her lyrics and her journey. They both idolized women like the Indigo Girls and celebrated at festivals like the Lilith Fair. They are part of a different time. Being gay, bisexual, binary, or anything in between, being just who you want to be was not accepted and not safe—it still isn't. I am not sure where my mom fell in the spectrum; all I know is that she was my mom. I will share the best I can, but there are factors I still don't understand to this day, just fractured memories and hidden truths.

My mom attended a Catholic school with nuns in shared very few details about this experience, but from it wasn't a good one. All she told me was that once she go high school, she believed all her new friends were damned was an extremely confusing time for her. And it was the reaso chose to raise us with strong moral values opposed to religious ones and to have an open mind and choose for ourselves.

She started dating my dad when she was sixteen and was from a town of 3,000. She travelled to Quebec as part of an exchange and got a taste for the world, a taste of her sense of self. Following that she married my dad when she was twenty-two and proceeded to have my brother, myself, and my sister shortly after. It was what was expected of her, and it was what she expected out of life—that's what she was taught. But then I think after the throes of the hustle and bustle of parenthood, and once we were school-aged, she started to find her sense of self again, and I think she realized it didn't quite fit and never had. Again, this is not my tale to tell and I can only guess. As a child I was oblivious and only now can reflect on the moments of her life.

It was actually in Halifax, along the same time in 2006 where I discovered Brandi Carlile in our tiny walk-in basement apartment, living with my new partner. He said, "My friend Jeff said your mom is a lesbian." I immediately said, "Well I don't think so," AND THAT HAD NEVER ACTUALLY OCCURRED TO ME until he just said it out loud to my face. I thought to myself, *Isn't that something I would know?!*

Later that evening memories came pelting down on me unexpectedly, like a hail storm in mid-summer. All at once flashing before my eyes and I thought, *Maybe she is.* I immediately called my brother and asked, "Is mom gay?" He said maybe, he didn't know, but it was highly possible. It so clearly had crossed his mind many years before that moment (as he is four years older and saw and processed so

..1 more than I did from our childhood). A lot more things made sense to me about my parents' separation and our upbringing. My parents are both kind and loving parents, and they did deeply care for one another; they were just better apart. They were victims of circumstances of their time and the experience of growing up in a small town with very little exposure to the outside world.

I mean, if I am really being honest with myself, and when I look back to when I was twenty-four and my mom made me watch all the seasons of "The L Word" with her, I think she was trying to expose me to something she didn't have when she was young. Maybe her way of saying, "Hello, there are more options for you and a diverse world out there for you; don't do what I did. Don't follow my path and don't limit yourself." She saw something in me that reminded her of herself and didn't want me to make the same mistakes she did. She was worried for me; I see that now. My sister told me that my mom once said when I was dating my partner, now husband, that I was "putting all my eggs in one basket."

She needn't have worried. I had found a kind and loving person. I fell in love with that person, my person. You just know, with every sense of yourself, that you are in love, and it is right, no matter their gender. In saying that, when society imposed that there was only one way to love and be loved, it was limited and simply narrow-minded. It is like saying there is one right skin colour, only one kind of music you can listen to, only one food you can eat, only one good flower that grows from the ground, only one way to sound when you speak, only one way to write—it's simply not the case. What has been limited are views: self-imposed, perpetuated through hate and fear.

The world is a variation of all things in nature, each person a unique blip in the insurmountable, vast universe in which we live surrounded by the stars. The stars, proof that our world is limitless and yet so small. We are tiny little Who-specks on a big universal flower.

Thinking about my mom and her journey now saddens me because I know she carried a heavy burden and could never fully express who she was. Because she felt it was not safe for her or her family. She sacrificed her whole life for her children because she thought it was the right thing to do at the time; she was scared. She was scared for us and of her very truths. I still wish it wasn't so; alas, I cannot turn back the hands of time. To me she could be gay, straight, and/or all that is in between, a yodelling enthusiast, the first woman on the moon—it didn't matter; to me, she was my mom. My heart. My home.

I wept on the way to Edmonton when hearing Brandi Carlile's journey—not the same as my mother's, but another's struggle to find her place in the world. And I wept the whole way home. Her story opened wounds in me about the loss of my mother I thought were long healed. I revisited childhood memories as Brandi sang about hers. I now know that I will never truly heal from this loss. The scars run so deep and will reopen from time to time.

My mom never shared parts of herself with us in order to protect us. I understand that now. I wish I could have known parts of her better. But I think this was her way of explaining that sacrifice. At my mom's wake, or "party," as she planned it before she passed, she requested we play "The Story," sung by Brandi Carlile and written by Phillip John Hanseroth.

All of these lines across my face
Tell you the story of who I am
So many stories of where I've been
And how I got to where I am

But these stories don't mean anything

When you've got no one to tell them to it's true
I was made for you.[15]

All We Can Do Is Keep On Living

As I put Finn to bed tonight, before he closed his sweet brown eyes rimmed with long lashes, he said, "Mom, I don't want to die." He says this every now and again, and it never gets any easier talking to him about it. Sometimes I think he is so in tune with his emotions that he can feel and exhibit my own. I tell him, "I know, I don't want you to die, and I never want to leave you, but one day I will die but still live; the way I keep on living is through you, just like you will live through your children." That is the best way I can describe it to them. Death is never easy but an inevitable fate.

Gus brought it up again at the dinner table. He said, "I want to live forever." I replied, "I don't think you do." Gus asked why, and I explained to him that at some point in your life you will get old (ideally) and you will get tired. You will be happy with the life you have had the chance to live. If we live forever, the sweetness of life would not be so sweet. That's why we have to be kind and love one another every day the best we can.

I slip on my slippers and head to my bed and reflect on these very emotional few hours. I know that I am where I am meant to be: in the family I have built with my partner. I speak about the loss of my mother and how it felt like I lost my sense of home. The thing is, I lost it, yes, but we stitched it back together; as a family, it's here again. She is still here in this home, but in a different way. She lives in the way I stroke my hand gently across my children's foreheads, she lives in the way I sound

---

[15] Brandi Carlile, "The Story," track 2 on *The Story*, Columbia Records, 2007, compact disc.

when I laugh, she lives in the way I love them in full sacrifice above my own being. She lives in the way I will live through them.

> *I am sure that the joy and pleasure they bring will far surpass any other of your life experiences.*
>
> – Love Grandma, Love Mom

Love

It is easy to forget, when we get wrapped up in the rigmarole of the day-to-day, that we need rest and connection. Sometimes the people we love the most we push away and are the hardest on. This is because we know they aren't going to leave—well, let's hope not anyway. There are moments when we can take our loved ones for granted, and even love itself for granted. And, alas, sometimes we wait until it's too late to let the people we love the most know how much we love them.

I grew up in a household that wasn't overly expressive and didn't give long-lasting hugs; my husband's family didn't show much public affection either. I've realized this and vowed to raise my family to give kisses and embrace and be open about expressing our emotions. It has been a really special gift, and a small unprompted "I love you" can literally lighten my whole day. My kids regularly state, "this is the best day of my life," and that reaffirms that I am doing something right—the floor may be covered in crap, toys, and garbage, but my kids are friggin' happy, and that IS something.

Same goes for your partner in crime. I know this is a different version of person for everyone, as all family units are completely unique, and not all families are blood-related. Tell the people who are a part of your unit, your day-to-day routines, that you appreciate them, that you love them, flaws and all. Because they need to hear it, and so do you. Risk being vulnerable, risk being seen, risk, risk, risk! Because all of those moments that add up, that is your life—the moments are your life. The people you see, yell at, interact with, lie with, kiss, hug, they are parts of your moments that add up to the person you want to be and the life you want to live.

No matter what our day entailed, my mother always had us meet for family dinners. We were torn away from whatever we were doing and sat down. It was routine and a way for our family to connect and be together. The way we interact with our loved ones has an insurmountable effect on their lives. You can shape other lives . . . isn't that one of the most beautiful and profound gifts?! Your family is your treasure, quirks and all. People are your home. People are the ones who pass on your memory. You live through others—that is your beautiful gift to this world.

Give Love & Take Love

Love conquers all—it is all that really matters in this world. Love is your legacy.

My brother—and poet, writer, and musician—Zachary Hofer wrote this for my mother after she passed:

> Inside of a boat on the top of the water. Our jigs are bouncing off of the bottom of the Beaver River and we are hauling fish into the boat at an incredible rate. In fact, we are catching them so fast that Uncle Bill doesn't have enough time to net everyone's fish, untangle our lines, and repair the motor quickly enough to drive us back up river, so we can drift back over the pickerel hole. The rain is driving sideways and the wind is picking up. Nobody in this boat gives a damn about the weather. . . . This is fishing.
>
> I am the firstborn "baby-boy" of "Donna." I am scared of my mom. She keeps me on my toes. I don't know whether

I am getting a delicious bowl of butterscotch pudding or some of Brandi's Gerber baby food, which is conveniently the same colour. I look into her eyes as I spoon the mystery substance towards my mouth. I study her expression, trying to get a hint of what I might be in for. I can never tell. She wears a cardplayer's face, and the only thing I know for sure is that she is thoroughly enjoying my predicament.

She shows me that things are not always as they seem. Donna—the sharp-witted, silver-tongued cardplayer, who, without saying a word, strikes fear into the hearts of my friends as they cautiously tiptoe through the entrance of our house—is not someone to be feared at all.

When I am lost, she holds steady, never showing the fear and worry I am sure lingers in every mother's mind. Her cardplayer's stone face becomes my rock, a steadiness I can hold on to. She is composed. Her dedication to her children never wavers. She has all of the answers and I learn quickly that she is never wrong.

As I get older, I begin to understand that the best argument is, in fact, no argument at all, as I stand no chance in hell of winning. I pass this knowledge on to Kayley and it helps her to lose many arguments faster and easier than ever before.

She sings "Phantom of the Opera" at the top of her lungs while making my favourite spaghetti. She talks on the phone constantly, planning a trip to the Lilith Fair, fishing, or the next Rod Stewart concert. I assume she is talking to her sisters, but when I ask her, she always says, " Oh, I was just talking to NONE OF YOUR BUSINESS!" She treasures her independence and I learn to do the same.

Brandi and Kayley stack the stairwell with stuffed animals and unroll every roll of toilet paper throughout the halls. Brandi is an aspiring artist; there is paint everywhere. Kayley picks out her own outfits, and when her head isn't stuck inside of her shirt, Brandi is giving her a haircut. There aren't many rules around our house, but everyone is treated with the respect and dignity we all deserve. There is no name-calling or telling someone to "shut up" or putting anyone down. These are the basic rules and you'd better not forget them.

These simple rules extend beyond the walls of our house. Donna is the resident troublemaker at her office. I watch the way her co-workers and clients revere and respect her opinions, and witness the excitement and sometimes bewilderment when she is around. She stages a protest at the lack of a dress code by wearing her own "Baby Tee belly baring shirt" to work. The results are shocking . . . Donna is right again.

She travels the world with her best friend. She is a sister, a daughter, a comedian, a friend, and a general. She walks around this room with the presence of a commanding officer. She is an old jackfish lurking in the weeds. She is the practical joke you wish you were clever enough to pull. She is the Five of Hearts and the Three of Spades. She is your most loyal friend and your fiercest protector, and above all of that, she is a mother, and you'd best not mess with any of her children. She is The Iotola, The Grand Poobah, The CHIEF!

She is our strength and resolve. She is our spiritual leader. She is Donnalyn KS Hofer, and magnificently she will sail, "Into the Mystic."

This was my mother, strong, quick-witted, and put her children and family at the forefront. We were her greatest sacrifice and win; I will forever be grateful. My mother gave us the beautiful gift of freedom and room to become who we were meant to be. She set us up for glory to the best of her abilities. We never had a lot of money, but we had love.

What is important, what matters most in this life, is the lives that you touch and impact.

Profound Moments

There is only one thing we can count on: one day we will die. That is a tough pill to swallow; no one likes to think about or acknowledge it, but it is part of our reality. Now, you can ask yourself, *What do I have to lose? What would life be without death*? A midst of grey, meaningless dribble. Alas, there must always be a balance.

Amongst the births of our first two children, I lost my mother and my husband lost his father. My mother had just over a year with us after she had learned about her illness. We lost my father-in-law, however, suddenly. But you know what the amazing thing about him was? It's kind of like he knew. Not like he knew—you never actually know—but he seemed like he didn't ever waste a moment. He lived his life grandly; he lived his life caring for others with all of his huge heart. He took the time with people, he asked questions, he listened intently, he made everyone feel at ease. You know how rare that is in a person? So much so, that we hear often of how Dwayne cared for other people and how he made them feel.

I recall being on holiday, and my first son Gus was about two, running around. From across the room I watched Dwayne (my father-in-law), and he was staring at Gus, his first and only grandchild, and tears were welling in his eyes. He came over to me and said, "You know, Brandi, this is what is important, right here; this is what life is all about." He gestured to Gus, his very first grandbaby and went over and embraced him in a bear hug.

He understood the vastness and complexities of how fragile and vital it is to live in this exact moment, the exact moment you were meant to be in right now. He knew. He lost his father when he was fourteen and he was the oldest of six siblings. He suffered one of those impactful moments in life that never leaves you; it moulded and shaped who he was. It was a loss that made him hyper-aware of how fleeting a precious moment can be, and how in an instant life can change. He carried that knowledge with him for all of the years following the loss of his own father. He was one of those people who radiates their own sunshine, and others cannot help but gravitate toward it.

I will always remember that moment and Dwayne's words. I will live my life with the awareness he himself lived by and passed on to me that day in the tiny café. Impactful moment. A tiny thread where his life connects to me, my husband, and my children.

Know that it is important to love, know that it is important to connect, know that it is important to live.

Tiny Threads

I hesitate to share this story with you now. It's difficult. Because our society judges. But we are human, we cannot do it all, and sometimes we screw up, big time. This particular event, however, is a crucial reminder to myself and others of the one and only truth we face: each and every life hangs on a tiny little thread.

It was a typical Sunday, the beautiful chaos of our lives with three boys six and under. We had a playdate planned for our afternoon and we were baking holiday cookies. Now, I was in charge of four busy boys and they were ripping through each level of our home. I yelled, "Okay, come down and decorate the cookies, everyone. Hey, Gus, where is Teddy?" Teddy poked his little head from upstairs and said, "Peekboo, Mom." So I asked Gus to go grab Teddy and bring him down to decorate cookies with us.

We carried on with the rest of the decorating, dinner, then bath and bed. I had a mastermind painting night online with a group of artists until 10 p.m. in my studio. Following that, I headed upstairs to bed and went to draw my bath in our master bathroom . . . only to find my bathroom ripped apart, everything off all the shelves, soaps, lotions, and *pills*! Pills everywhere! *No no no!* I thought to myself. I dragged my hands over my tired face and roughly through my unwashed hair. I called my husband in. He was worried; I could see it in his face, drained of blood and pale white with worry. Teddy had gone through all the pills.

I immediately called poison control. She asked what he had gotten into. Tylenol—not good. But they were the white ones; not tasty at all. She said that was good; I was quite certain he hadn't eaten these. But I could only find two on the floor and the woman from poison control said he needed to have ingested six to eight, and with Tylenol the response has a twelve-hour delay and then his liver could shut down and he would need a transplant; okay, that cannot be not our only option here. Even if I was quite sure he didn't eat any, we were not risking it, not when the alternative is a slow wait until it's too late. By this time, it was almost 11. We woke up Teddy and packed him up and I headed with him to the ER.

And before you judge us, we got locking cabinets the day before because the boys like to get into everything, and I mean everything. I hadn't yet locked up that one bottle . . . it was almost empty and so high out of his reach, or so I thought. . . .

From making potions to flushing balls and tampons down the toilet, nothing is off-limits to these children, or any children, for that matter. Teddy can climb, crib hop, drawer scale, clamber up kitchen cabinets, and, in this case, tackle 7 feet up on the very top of a bathroom cabinet. He is also Harry friggin' Houdini. I wish I could watch him every second of every day, but it is humanly impossible. I have two other children who also require my attention, not to mention all the other tasks I manage in a day. So, this happened. I wish it hadn't. But it did. The unimaginable happened.

We arrived and they got us in right away. Nevertheless, it was three very long hours, attempting to get a two-year-old to stay on a hospital cot inside a curtained room, with worried thoughts racing through my mind. I pulled out my phone and little Teddy and I proceeded to watch all the family videos. He was so sweet and laid with me, giggling and adding little comments along the way.

However, watching our lives flash before my eyes, I just thought, *My Teddy, not my Teddy. What have I done? I can't lose my sweet, sweet baby boy.* I was weeping. Since he arrived, he has graced our lives with an uninhibited amount of joy. He hugs strangers and has this way of winning over every heart he comes across. Yes, our lives have been out of control since this little guy came along, but we could not imagine our lives without him. His brother Finn reserves only the sweetest disposition for Teddy alone and has loved him since they first laid eyes on one another. Finn loved him so much as a chubby babe that he kept biting him; not in the way you would think, he just was so full of love he would smother, kiss, coo, and bite baby Teddy because he couldn't find a way to express just how much he loved him.

They tested Teddy's levels and after what seemed like the longest hours of my life, the doctor walked in and said we were good. He didn't eat the bottle of Tylenol. We drove home on the desolate winter night back to our beds at 3 a.m. We rested, knowing that the worst could have happened and it didn't. We kissed our sweet Teddy goodnight, in peace, knowing he was safe.

My mom said to me once that there is no greater loss than the loss of a child. I experienced a pin drop of that emotion that evening at the hospital. I vowed to be grateful for this gift of life, always.

Where did all the Tylenol end up, you ask? Two months later I found it dumped into a toothpaste box at the back of my cabinet.

Impactful Moments

Impactful moment: a moment that holds momentous reason; a moment that can change your life as you know it.

When your baby gets laid on your chest and he is breathing and crying and real. The moment that holds so much joy and relief and reminds you what it really is to be alive.

When everyone tells you that you're in love, you just know, and you experience that very first kiss that made you understand what they really meant.

When we get caught in the rigamarole of all the small things, we can sometimes forget what a miracle it takes for us to be here every day. There is nothing more extraordinary than the simple fact that we are alive and will one day cease to exist. It is a delicate balance in which we hang on the edge.

The last eve of my mother's life seems a faraway memory. I keep it locked. Buried deep. Recalling fierce emotion, an erupting wound that refuses to clot, leaking blood, with no resolution in sight.

The events of that evening happened to another person of another time. When I play them like a rolling reel in my mind, it is like witnessing a stranger in that room with her. I remember everyone's clothes, my red skirt, the wood panelling in the hospital elevator after we left, the plaid shirt draped on top of my mother's body. I'm sure we were all strangers in our own bodies that night. The events burned into our memories that we all avoid with all our efforts and mental power in order to carry on living our own lives. For who can constantly bear the burden of thoughts of the un-evadable balance to life: death.

There we were, a family, strangers in a room, hovering above, witnessing death in an out-of-body experience. For we were not ourselves in that moment; we didn't know who we were, trapped in a heavily wrapped cocoon of emotions that demanded to be felt, no escape in sight. We sang for lack of knowing what to say or do. We sang to her one very last time, together.

We walked in unison out of the room to see the nurse weeping at her desk. She wept at the beauty of it all, as a witness to how a family could love one another so deeply, the only way to express themselves and comfort their mother in the last minutes she had in her body was through song. Our hearts beat as one.

The moment I held my mom's hand and knew that life had left it—the same hand that had comforted me in all my times of sorrow—her hand was still. I held onto it. The hand that had rested on my back as a wailing babe. The hand that fastened the button to my dress on my wedding day. The hand that dealt out countless hands of cards with a tumbler jar of red wine next to it. The hand that gently caressed my hair as I lay my head in her lap as a child. All I could think about was her hand. I stared at it, knowing my life would never be the same after I let it go. It wasn't. It never could be.

I recall laying in the foetal position on the shag carpet of our living room. Clutching my swollen, pregnant belly and weeping; the baby would not stop stirring. How could this baby deal with the intense amount of emotion and grief? I felt like I could never recover from this intense loss. Something had been stripped away that I could never prepare for. A thread tethered and severed, no longer holding me to my mother. I was at a loss and helpless. My mind was searching and searching to find a solution to stop feeling this immense and unbearable pain. A hamster wheel of thoughts turning and turning as I was wreathed in and overcome by grief.

Yet somehow, unexpectedly, through the throes of grief, I found strength. Strength for my own newborn baby when I held him in my arms, Gus. I had been presented with the highest form of gift. That I will hold in my own hands the small joys, the small moments, the moments that add up to a lifetime of love. My mother could never be replaced, but she lived on through me, and she will live on through my children.

My hands have purpose now, just as my mother's did, just as her mother's did and hers before that. Gus always longed to be held, and I was happy to oblige. Sleeping through many nights as his tiny hand clutched my finger or his head lay on my chest and our hearts beat as one. Finn's soft cheek is always nuzzling my palm as he once again declares that he loves me the most. My hands gently stroke the soft skin of Teddy's eyelids, my last baby, as I sing him a quiet lullaby and whisper the secret I reserve only for them—that every parent knows—there is nothing in this world you could ever love more.

Our love, our compassion for our children is a power capable of saving humanity; women full of compassion and love and empathy, we are the key. Women are the salvation for the world. I know it in my heart.

> *"We are here to fully introduce ourselves, to impose ourselves and ideas and thoughts and dreams onto the world, leaving it*

changed forever by who we are and what we bring forth from our depths. So we cannot contort ourselves to fit into the visible order. We must unleash ourselves and watch the world reorder itself in front of our eyes."[16]

– Glennon Doyle

With my three boys who are now seven, five, and two, everything is flying by in a blur, like race cars in a rainbow of colour zooming past your face. Every moment is an adventure as I witness things for the very first time through their eyes. Life moves in sporadic, unpredictable, emotionally charged events that lie in the hands of my tiny humans, who can, at the drop of the hat, make you roll over in laughter or weep from the exhaustion of it all. A rollercoaster I gladly hop on at 6 a.m. every day. Not knowing what highs and lows are to come until the very last moment, when everything plummets into the depth, taking hold of every fracture of your being, reminding you of the all-consuming exhilarating fact that YOU ARE ALIVE.

A very wise woman said to me once:

The only thing I know for certain is that the sun will rise and set; the rest is beyond my control.

– My mom's older sister, and my Aunty Gwen

I am finishing here today with you. Reading these final moments on the eighth anniversary of my mother's passing. The timing of it all seems a bit odd—how, on this day, am I finally reading these last words to you? But in the same breath, not odd at all. I was meant to be here. I was meant to feel all of this. To process the moments of my life and grow as

[16] Glennon Doyle, *Untamed* (New York: Penguin Random House, 2020), 66.

a human, as a woman. A women who has been unleashed by revealing herself to the world.

The Stars

My new friend, I thank you for your time and appreciate your being here with me for my very first book. I want you to know just how unique and special you really are. Did you know it takes a star's light more than 100 years to reach our night sky? By the time a star burns out, we wouldn't know until years and years later, and each star is its own solar system? And our Milky Way galaxy is just one of a billion galaxies in our system? I read that in one of my children's books. Those are just things we know. What about what we don't know yet? That alone lights my brain on fire! There are things around us that we can feel, but we cannot fully fathom, and that does not scare me . . . it excites me, as it should you!

Now, let's just think about the absolutely amazing fact that you and I are here right now, and what it took for that to happen. I mean, just the simple fact that I am me, and that you are you, and out of all the cosmos and generations and occurrences your parents met and theirs and theirs and so on and so forth (and all the other stuff we don't think about our parents doing but needs to be brought up to make my point), and the one sperm met the one egg and you came out a pure miracle (one of life's greatest), a screaming ball of life and energy, and I grew into me and you grew into you. What are the odds that we are both alive and here right now? I am no math expert, but I am going to ballpark it and say infinite.

The universe, or your version of the way we are all connected, made you. You! Out of infinite possibilities! You were meant to be here right now, in the form you are in, for a spectacular reason. The world, the universe, the cosmos wants to see you shine your brightest! Believe—believe that you were made with purpose, because you were. You were not only made with purpose, but you came into a world filled with endless possibilities. There are stars dancing around you filled with ideas, choices, and opportunities. Look around, behold them, observe them in wonder. You are a gift, and the world is on your side; listen to it, feel it, and bask in all its glory that you simply exist.

Trust me, I used to think this was all some weird magic hippie talk; however, my life shifted. With that shift I came to realize that the universe and the world did, after all, have my back. The more I put myself out there, the more the proof was there, simply by the decision to accept there is something magical happening all around me. It became harder and harder to ignore.

This all started after the loss of my mother. She had this thing about dimes. "They are a sign," she would always say and hold it up wherever she found one. I thought, *Cool, Mom, go add it to your dime collection.* Since her passing, everyone in our inner circle of family and friends keeps getting "dimed." And every time we do, we send one another a picture of where we found our dime that day.

Our family friend Veena got up off of her massage table once and the masseuse picked something off her back. It was a dime, stuck to her back. My cleaner, Wilma, started finding them all around our house, and she eventually found so many dimes she put them in a jar for us and labeled it "Dimes from Mom." I still have it, and it is full. They pop up when I need them, like a little reminder: "You've got this," or, "You're on the right track," or, "You're where you're meant to be."

When I painted my first 50-foot mural there was a dime waiting for me by my truck door on the wet pavement on a rainy day. I plucked it out of the water and smiled. I was recently the best man for my mom's best friend, Philip, on his wedding day. As they were moving through the ceremony I thought, *Oh my gosh, I need a dime for when we welcome Aaron* [his new husband] *to our family.* I thought to myself, *Gee, I hope I have one.* After the ceremony I went and grabbed my wallet out of my handbag and opened it to find no money inside except for one single dime. That dime said, "Hey, it's Mom, I am here to celebrate my best friend's wedding!" If that is not universal intelligence or intuition or god or magic or faith, I don't know what is. The more I believe, the more I find proof. Just yesterday I found a curled-over, bent dime. I'm not sure what that meant . . . maybe "finish your damn book already; it's time?" Or "Have a nap with your baby . . ." THAT I did; I curled up for a Teddy snuggle right beside our fire where I found said dime.

The more you believe you were brought into this world for a purpose, the more you will realize you are in charge of your own destiny. I didn't get it then, but my mom kept saying that phrase over and over in the month before she passed: "You are in charge of your own destiny." I finally feel it. I finally see it. I find dimes all over the place as reminders that we are still tethered to one another, just in a different way—it will never be broken. And I know, I just know, that you will feel yours and you will see yours too. I have faith in you, my friend, for you are in charge of your own destiny.

Seeing Your Everyday Ordinary As Extraordinary

What I have shared with you here is, in my experience, the way to move forward in the life you see for yourself, the life that YOU CHOOSE. It took me a while to get here, not that we ever arrive anywhere. However, I have arrived at a point where I can share with gratitude and pride parts of my life that have gotten me here. There is no greater joy than to know that you can empower others to find that magic within themselves, to see their days as truly extraordinary.

You may not look around and see what you want to see or be present in what is happening to you right now. If that is so, through appreciation for where you are, who you are, where you came from, what you've already done, through appreciation and acceptance of those life lessons, the building blocks and foundations of what you can become, know they were all for a reason. Know that every moment you live is a worthy moment, just as you are; your everyday life is extraordinary, just as you are equally extraordinary. I see you, and you are abundantly beautiful. I cannot wait for you to share every part of yourself with the world.

Thank you for your time. I sure appreciate you giving me just a little bit of it.

BIOGRAPHY

Brandi Hofer

Brandi Hofer is an artist, muralist, author, podcaster, educator, and founder of the Colour Me Happy Community.

Brandi is most well-known for being a successful collected Canadian Artist, exhibiting internationally and across North America. In 2021, she was featured by *Create! Magazine* in their article "28 Contemporary Artists You Need To Know About." Her podcast, *Colour Me Happy!*, has garnered attention as one of the best art podcasts to binge this season by *Create! Magazine*.

Brandi's artwork has been featured on national television and can be found in international publications. She has experience in creating custom artworks for designers and translates her artwork into large-scale murals. Brandi has attended creative residencies at Red Deer College; Toronto Island; the Marnay Art Centre outside Paris, France; and in Montreal, Quebec. Her work has appeared in HGTV's *House of Bryan* and was featured in a General Motors commercial, and her family appeared at their in-home art studio for an international commercial for Walmart.

Most recently Brandi will be founding an Art academy in her local public school system for young people to connect to their creative selves through: art therapy, outdoor learning, community outreach, and public art.

Brandi continues to inspire and share in her journey with the world through many creative mediums. Brandi Hofer's studio, where she works and creates with her children, is located in the Canadian prairies.

Leah Dunkheld

Leah is a thirteen-year-old illustrator at the cusp of her creative career and was asked by Brandi to create illustrations for her book. Her illustrations went above and beyond all expectations, and she will do great things in this world.

Thank you to:

My partner and husband, who made the most amazing dad. You are the person who I have always leaned on and you've always held me.

My very special family, unique, creative, and full of love and compassion. All of them (and there are many) who have been the biggest support over the years. A wholehearted thank you—I am the luckiest person on Earth.

My mother-in-law, who has the most of my paintings, and always lets me paint her beautiful face. My children are very lucky to have such a special Maman.

My Dad, there is so much to say that I would need another book. But, Dad, you are kind and you're the BEST Grandpa.

My friend and Studio Manager Jenni, for believing in me more than anyone else, and also for listening to me talk more than anyone else.

Stephanie Carbajal for being the greatest, most dedicated, and thorough editor and helping me through this first book of mine. I had no clue what I was doing. Let's face it—this book is an expressive abstract painting and it needed to be sorted through so others could read and understand it!

Sheila Bouchard for taking on more and more editing, and for the friendship over the years.

Leah Dunkheld for being the coolest, most talented and driven thirteen-year-old young woman I've ever met.

Jeff, my neighbor, for I was not only just jealous of him for writing a book, but also lucky enough to be coached by him through the whole publishing process, from start to finish. His book is amazing: *Clone Yourself: Build a Team that Understands Your Vision, Shares Your Passion, and Runs Your Business For You*—find it on Amazon!

And most of all, thank you all for being here.

READING RECOMMENDATIONS

Here is a link to Oliver Burkeman's last article in the *Guardian* that I mentioned, it's a great one!
https://www.theguardian.com/lifeandstyle/2020/sep/04/oliver-burkemans-last-column-the-eight-secrets-to-a-fairly-fulfilled-life

Here is a list of my favourite Jen Sincero books:

Badass Habits: Cultivate the Awareness, Boundaries, and Daily Upgrades You Need to Make Them Stick

You Are a Badass at Making Money: Master the Mindset of Wealth

You Are a Badass Every Day: How to Keep Your Motivation Strong, Your Vibe High, and Your Quest for Transformation Unstoppable

You Are a Badass: How to Stop Doubting Your Greatness and Start Living an Awesome Life

The Dark by Lemony Snicket is the book that I love to read to my children.

One of the most valuable books I've ever read for getting children on the go in a fun way was *The Happiest Toddler on the Block* by Harvey Karp.

The most interesting and effective book I have read on creating and maintaining habits is *Atomic Habits* written by James Clear—it is wildly popular!

BIBLIOGRAPHY

Burkeman, Oliver. "Oliver Burkeman's last column: the eight secrets to a (fairly) fulfilled life." *Guardian*, September 4, 2020. https://www.theguardian.com/lifeandstyle/2020/sep/04/oliver-burkemans-last-column-the-eight-secrets-to-a-fairly-fulfilled-life.

Carlile, Brandi. *The Story*. 2007. Columbia Records. Compact disc.

Carrey, Jim. 2014. Transcript of commencement speech delivered at the Maharishi University of Management, May 30, 2014. https://www.rev.com/blog/transcripts/jim-carrey-commencement-speech-transcript-2014-at-maharishi-university-of-management.

Curtis, Richard, dir. *About Time.* Universal City, CA: Universal Pictures, 2013. 2 hr., 3 min.

Docter, Pete and Kemp Powers, dirs. *Soul.* Emeryville, CA: Pixar Animation Studios, 2020. 1 hr., 49 min. https://www.disneyplus.com/movies/soul/77zlWrb9vRYp.

Doyle, Glennon. *Untamed.* New York: Penguin Random House, 2020.

Gilbert, Elizabeth. *Big Magic.* New York: Penguin Random House, 2015.

lang, k.d. 2013. Transcript of speech delivered at the Juno Awards of 2013 at the Brandt Centre, Regina, Saskatchewan, April 20, 2013. https://www.huffpost.com/archive/ca/entry/kd-lang-juno-speech-2013_n_3129280.

Roosevelt, Theodore. "Citizenship in a Republic." 1910. Transcript of speech delivered at the Sorbonne in Paris, France, April 23, 1910. https://www.presidency.ucsb.edu/documents/address-the-sorbonne-paris-france-citizenship-republic.

Sincero, Jen. *You Are a Badass at Making Money*. New York: Penguin Random House, 2017.

Snicket, Lemony. *The Dark*. New York: Little Brown and Company, 2013.

Wattles, Wallace D. *The Science of Getting Rich*. CreateSpace Independent Publishing Platform, 2017.

YOU CAN FIND US IN OUR FREE COMMUNITY ON FACEBOOK AND INSTAGRAM:
COLOUR ME HAPPY COMMUNITY

LISTEN TO OUR PODCAST:
COLOUR ME HAPPY! HOSTED BY BRANDI HOFER STUDIOS ON ALL PODCAST PLATFORMS AND YOUTUBE

LEARN FROM US:
WWW.BRANDIHOFER.CA/CMHLEARN

FIND OUT MORE:
WWW.BRANDIHOFER.CA

SAVE $10 ON ALL OUR ART PRODUCTS AND CLASSES!
USE CODE: LOVE AT CHECKOUT

Thanks friend!

WE WOULD LOVE TO HEAR FROM YOU!

WE ALL KNOW NOW THAT KINDNESS TAKES A LOT LESS ENERGY!

SPREAD EVEN MORE LOVE AND HELP US GROW BY LEAVING A HEARTFELT REVIEW ON AMAZON.

SHARE IT, GIFT IT, HELP SOMEONE ELSE TO SEE THIER EVERYDAY ORDINARY AS EXTRAORDINARY!

ALL THE LOVE,
XOXO

BRANDI

Manufactured by Amazon.ca
Bolton, ON